SNAKEBIRD
THIRTY YEARS OF ANHINGA POETS

2004

SNAKEBIRD
THIRTY YEARS OF ANHINGA POETS

Edited by
Rick Campbell
& C. L. Knight

2004

Cover art and design, book design, and production – C.L. Knight
Typesetting – Titles set in Microgramma; text set in Adobe Garamond

Library of Congress Cataloging-in-Publication Data
Snakebird – Thirty Years of Anhinga Poets
Edited by Rick Campbell and C. L. Knight – First Edition
ISBN 0938078-79-8
Library of Congress Card Number: 2004100005

This publication is sponsored in part by a grant from the
Florida Department of State, Division of Cultural Affairs,
and the Florida Arts Council.

Our thanks to the Stuckey Foundation for its generous support.

Anhinga Press Inc. is a nonprofit corporation dedicated
wholly to the publication and appreciation of fine poetry.

For personal orders, catalogs and information write to:
Anhinga Press
P.O. Box 10595
Tallahassee, FL 32302
Web site: www.anhinga.org
E-mail: info@anhinga.org

Published in the United States
by Anhinga Press
Tallahassee, Florida
First Edition, 2004

For Van K. Brock
Founder of Anhinga Press

PRELUDE TO THE VOYAGE

So I have begun telling the world I am leaving it,
even giving them the name of the famous spaceship
scheduled for the furtherest galaxies, through wormholes,
through timewarps, past points of no return. Everyone
must know and many will think I am mad, many closest
to me. Perhaps I am even glad, always a Macadamian,
the country where I am normal, always ready to turn
the world upside down. Perhaps you too wonder, think
I'm odd. Yes, aren't we, Pistachio, you of the mysterious
center — pink, green, salty stranger I caught in thought
among the flowers in the garden of the sighted and
the garden of the blind, whose perfections and incongruities,
of laughter and quiet solemnity are sought and treasured.
And we walked to the Greyhound cafeteria at midnight,
the city closed down, the unhoused and unhouseled sleeping
on surrounding sidewalks. And you showed me the cool
cathedral of San Fernando in the scorching summer,
where San Martin de Porres, the first black saint (barber,
farm laborer), stood, friend of the los perros de Lima,
devoted to penances. He also flew through the air, stood in two
places at once, solved dilemmas for the wise. From him
I have learned there are no mysteries nature does not mimic,
no miracles without seeds in earth and water, wind and sky.
Goodbye, goodbye. I am leaving. I hope to see you there.

— Van K. Brock

CONTENTS

ACKNOWLEDGMENTS

The editors thank these publications where selected poems first appeared.

JAMES BROCK
> "Killing the Exotics," *Gulfstream*
> "Upon Hearing That My Grant Application Was Passed Over and the Winner Was a Bio-tech Professor Who Has Designed Genetically-altered Protein For Buckwheat Seed," *Caffeine Destiny*

VAN K. BROCK
> "Rouault," *The New Yorker*
> "Chagall among Developers," *The American Voice*
> "The Hindenberg," *The New England Review/ Bread Loaf Quarterly*
> "Buchenwald" and "The Nightmare: Ruth," *Crazy Horse 15*
> "Leaf Song," *Poets in the South: Conversations Within the Word*
> "Christ in the Sun," *Skullpolish* and *The Hard Essential Landscape* (Contemporary Poetry Series: University of Central Florida, University Presses of Florida, 1980)
> "Island of Paradise," *Quarterly Review of Literature*

FLEDA BROWN
> "Delaware," *Prairie Schooner*
> "Water Rising," *The Southern Review*

DONALD CASWELL
> "44 Quarters," *Your Grace*
> "Ars Poetica" and "In the Style of Tu Fu at Christmas Time in Kansas City," *The Same*
> "High, Inside Fastball," *Poetry*
> "Teachers," *The Boy That Was Made Out of Wood* (Wellberry Press, 1991)

MARY ANN COLEMAN

>The editors wish to thank Stephen Corey for finding and selecting
>Ms. Coleman's poems.

"Still Life with Rain and Nectarines," "Leanings," "The
Burning," and "On Watching *The Martian
Chronicles*," *Recognizing the Angel* (The Press of the
Nightowl, 1991)

"The Day Mother Buttered Her Purse," *Secret Passageway*
(Agee Publishers, Inc., 1988)

"On Watching *The Martian Chronicles*" and "The Burning,"
Lullwater Review

"Leanings," *The Remington Review*

"Still Life with Rain and Nectarines," *Negative Capability*

GARY CORSERI

"Bamboo Women," *The Open Cell*

"An Amaranth for Chico," *City Lights Review*

"Aunt Gianetta, at 80," *Sparrow*

"Hsieh Ho Explains His Art," *Madison Review*

"On a Print by Hiroshige," *The Georgia Review*

"Getting Sentimental," *A Local Muse*

"Once in Japan," *National Forum*

"Por los Niños," *Bloomsbury Review*

ROBERT DANA

"The Gill Netters," *The Southern California Anthology*

"At Seventy," *The Georgia Review*

"The Knot," *The Chariton Review*

"Fireworks," *The North American Review*

FRANK X. GASPAR

"Winter Berries," *Hudson Review*

"Stealing," *Tampa Review*

"Field Guide to the Heavens," *A Field Guide to the Heavens*
(University of Wisconsin Press, 1999)

"Hobbes," *The Georgia Review* and *Night of a Thousand Blossoms* (Alice James Books, 2004)
"The Holyoke," *The Holyoke* (Northeastern University Press, 1989) and *New England Review*
"It is the Nature of the Wing," *Harvard Review* and *Night of a Thousand Blossoms* (Alice James Books, 2004)

LOLA HASKINS
"The .38," *Southern Review*
"Times," *The Georgia Review*
"The Sand Hill Cranes," *The God Particle*
"Nana," *Mothering*

JANET HOLMES
"Celebration on the Planet Mars," *Humanophone* (University of Notre Dame Press, 2001)

DAVID KIRBY
"Your Momma Says Omnia Vincit Amor," *Big Leg Music* (Orchises Press, 1995), Used by permission of the author and Ochises Press

JUDITH KITCHEN
"Bahia de Todos os Santos," *Distance and Direction* (Coffee House Press, 2001) and *Green Mountains Review* (under the title, "Octet: Brazil")
"Sonora," *Distance and Direction* (Coffee House Press, 2001) and *Great River Review*

P. V. LEFORGE
"Golfin' Matilda," *Getting a Good Read*
"The Dirt Eaters," *Nimrod*

MIA LEONIN

"Drought," *Prairie Schooner*

"Mojo," *Transom*

"The Repeating Garden" and "How the Braiding Began,"
Indiana Review

JULIA B. LEVINE

"Mercy," *Ploughshares*

"Black Wheel," *Eckerd College Review*

"The Vanishing Point," *Ask* (University of Tampa Press, 2003)

RICK LOTT

"Blue Rain in the New World" and "Here in Emerald City,"
Southern Review

ERIKA MEITNER

"Kinky," *The Paterson Literary Review*

"Elegy," *The Southern Review*

JUDSON MITCHAM

"Notes for a Prayer in June" and "The Touch," *Somewhere in
Ecclesiastes* (University of Missouri Press, 1991)

JEAN MONAHAN

"Quitting Coffee" and "Lessons of the Eye Teeth,"
Believe It or Not (Orchises Press, 1998)
Used by permission of the author and Ochises Press
"Woman Falls Asleep Doing the Sunday Crossword," and "The
Kiss," *Same Difference*

MICHAEL MOTT

"August, Alceste," *Visions*

"Piano at Midnight," *Tar River Poetry*

"Not-so-secret Lives: Homage to Tissot," *The Sewanee Review*

ANN NEELON
"World Series," *The Gettysburg Review*
"Today at Marche Sandaga," *Ironwood*

NAOMI SHIHAB NYE
"Cinammon Twist," *Natural Bridge*
"Mint Snowball," *Never in a Hurry: Essays on People & Places,*
(University of South Carolina Press, 1996)
"How to Get There" was first read on National Public Radio.

RICARDO PAU-LLOSA
"Ostiones y Cangrejos Moros,"*New England Review* and *Cuba*
(Pittsburgh: Carnegie-Mellon University Press, 1993)
"Maya Corridor," *Vereda Tropical* (Pittsburgh: Carnegie-Mellon
University Press, 1999)
"Sorting Metaphors," *Poetry Northwest*
"Red Hole" and "Paris Inundated," *Kayak*
"Terraces," *Michigan Quarterly Review*

FRANCIS POOLE
"A Box Car," *Blades*
"Rising Early the Last Day of October," *Black Moon*

KEITH RATZLAFF
"Jubilate," *The Georgia Review*
"Howling Dog," *Poetry Northwest*

SHERRY RIND
"Wish for a Bare Desk," *A Fall Out the Door*
(Confluence Press, 1994)
"Basic Research," *Seattle Review*
"Food Chain," *Puerto del Sol*

YVONNE SAPIA
"English Only!" *Karamu*
"These are My Ghosts," *Eclipse*

LEON STOKESBURY
"Evening's End," "Unsent Message to My Brother in His Pain,"
and "Day Begins at Governors Square Mall," *Autumn
Rhythm: New and Selected Poems* (University of
Arkansas Press, 1996)
"Listening to My Mother's Comic Banter with Sackboys
and Servers," *The Kenyon Review*

JULIA M. SULLIVAN
Drawing: Anhinga with passage from St. John Perse

KATHLEEN WAKEFIELD
"Morning Glories," *The Georgia Review*
"Lines for My Father," *The Journal*

PATTI WHITE
"Billy Bailey Executed at 12:04 AM," *Nimrod International
Journal*

MICHELE WOLF
"Oranges," *Poetry in Performance 28*
"Toilette," *The Hudson Review*
"Artificial Breathing," *The Ledge*
"The Midnight Crossing," *Poet Lore*
"Pocono Lakeside," *Poetry*
"The Great Tsunami," *Mercy of Tides: Poems for a Beach House*
(Salt Marsh Pottery Press, 2003), *Proposing on the
Brooklyn Bridge* (Grayson Books, 2003), and *Poetry*

Memories of the Origin of Anhinga Press

Anhinga began in 1974. Always a variety of volunteers helped create the books.[1] Anhinga was first formed to publish the best representative poems by the children in the Poets-in-the-Schools program I helped launch in Florida and ran in Tallahassee. The object of publishing them was to show what children could do and to validate the program. The proceeds from the books helped publish other poets in Tallahassee. *A Spot of Purple is Deaf* had the first Anhinga imprint. The title was from a poem by Eddie Robinson, a student in my son's fourth grade class. *Lime Tree Prism,* first of the children's books was published by Apalachee Poetry Center. I chose the name Anhinga shortly afterward and *Lime Tree Prism* was distributed as an Anhinga book. Francis Poole and I edited both books together.

The Anhinga (*anhinga anhinga*) has been called a freshwater cormorant, but it is found in fresh, salt, and brackish water and, unlike the cormorant, it never evolved oil ducts. To dry, it perches with wings spread. Seemingly unpoetic, black with white markings, the Anhinga flies well and swims both on and under water. With its body submerged and long neck raised like a periscope as it swims, Indians called it "Snakebird." Perched, with white markings like lightning on its spread wings, it was Thunderbird. The Anhinga can disappear under water and re-surface fifty yards away. A bird full of metaphor and mystery, with its knowledge of heights and depths and its dramatic surfaces, seemed a fitting namesake for a poetry press.

The Anhinga, inhabiting coastal areas from North America to South America, was distinctive but not narrowly regional. It was Donald Caswell, one of the first poets published, who helped me now and then from the beginning of the press, who found St. John Perse's passage about the Anhinga that we used in a logo on the back of some of the early chapbooks.[2]

When I came to Florida State University in 1970 to help launch a graduate creative writing program, literate voices had been stomped on when, to oppose late 1960s student activism related to the VietNam "conflict," the president of the university abolished the long respected *Florida Flambeau* daily newspaper and the historic literary magazine,

The Legend. The *Flambeau,* the best newspaper in town at the time, survived by selling ads, but the literary journal died permanently. The university president was replaced, and though the first amendment was once again tolerated, the university continued in anxiety. Such things made something like Anhinga seem necessary.

Eventually, with the help of student writers, I published an anthology of poems by poets emerging from the Writing Program, along with poets who taught in the program or had visited it from elsewhere;[3] then an anthology from a Florida Poets-in-the-Prisons program I ran;[4] and chapbooks by three outstanding undergraduate poets and a young professor who had begun publishing poems.[5]

After several other chapbooks,[6] we published the full-length poetry book, *Counting the Grasses,*[7] by British-American writer Michael Mott. Next, I wanted to make Anhinga a regular publisher of poets in English, regardless of their location. After much discussion of these goals with Donald Caswell, we decided to start the annual Anhinga Prize for Poetry, which Donald directed out of my office at first, and then out of his home. I asked William Stafford to select the first winner, who turned out to be from Miami — Ricardo Pau-Llosa, an excellent poet whose publication both focused and widened our scope. Donald continued as primary director until 1988, when I resumed direction of the press, for which board member, attorney, and poet Steven Huss had gained non-profit status.

Many others deserve praiseworthy mention, but increasingly poet Rick Campbell directed Anhinga outstandingly. His multi-faceted and professional board partners with outstanding writers elsewhere — such as their agreement with Fresno State University for Anhinga to publish the Levine Prize winner. The Anhinga Prize is now highly regarded. And with help from the Florida Arts Council, the press is able to regularly publish books by Florida poets through its Florida Poetry Series.

So, Anhinga continues to serve a local poetry community while including outstanding poets from far off. There are many whose contributions Rick and I both cherish. Lynne Knight and Laura Sullivan are among these. Having personally done much of the layout and design for a number of Anhinga Poetry Prize books, I was most happy when Lynne and others, with their professional graphics excellence, took over the design chores. I met a poet three weeks ago whose immediate response on hearing Anhinga Press, was that it published beautiful books — inside and out.

One hopes an enterprise like Anhinga Press will continue. I want to say it stands on its own, but it doesn't. It is fortunate in the quality of the board which helps sustain it. I see much good that Rick has done, that I did not.

A few years ago Anhinga poets had their own poetry reading section at the Associated Writing Programs conference in Albany, NY. All who read thought it was as good a reading as they had participated in, and many who attended, not knowing Anhinga previously, had a similar perception. From the proofs I have seen, and knowing most of these poets, I think the reader of *Snakebird* will see why.

> — *Van K. Brock*
> *January 2004*
> *Rabun Gap, Georgia*

A Note on the Anhinga Prize for Poetry

When Van Brock and I introduced the Anhinga Prize for Poetry competition in 1983, Van had already taken Anhinga a long way from its beginning as publisher of student anthologies. A series of chapbooks by promising young local poets was followed by Michael Mott's *Counting the Grasses*, a writer who was neither local nor a novice.

Anhinga enjoyed an excellent reputation among local and regional writers. We hoped that the Anhinga Prize competition would expand both Anhinga's pool of talented writers and its audience, while allowing us to continue to publish local and regional poets.

Because neither of us had experience administering a competition, I suggested we test the waters by offering a statewide competition for a chapbook. The results of that enterprise were Cynthia Cahn's *The Day the Sun Split*, chosen by Leon Stokesbury, and a firm conviction on my part that the Anhinga Prize competition would fulfill our expectations.

It did. We received a mountain of manuscripts, which an army of volunteer readers whittled down to 20 for our judge, William Stafford. He made his choice quickly — a good thing, because other publishers were whittling away at our finalists. Because the judging process took several months, before we were done, some of each year's finalists were chosen for other national prizes — the Walt Whitman, AWP, and Samuel French Morse prizes, among others.

Clearly, we were getting manuscripts from some of the best poets writing in English, and though our audience didn't grow as rapidly as our submissions, we were gaining a national reputation. My only regret was that too many commitments caused me to end the Florida Chapbook competition after its second winner was named — Yvonne Sapia's *The Fertile Crescent*, chosen by Peter Meinke.[8]

In its twenty years, the Anhinga Prize's reputation has grown along with the reputations of its winners. Anhinga Prize winners have gone on to publish other books of poetry and win more prizes. Some have published prose — criticism, fiction, and memoir. Their works appear regularly in the most distinguished literary publications — *Poetry, Georgia Review, Southern Review, Ploughshares,* and *New England Review,* among others. I feel honored to have played a small part in bringing their early work to the public.

With the Anhinga Prize celebrating its twentieth winner and the Press its thirtieth year, Anhinga has surely come of age. This anthology is a tribute to the volunteer staff that has managed to keep Anhinga alive for three decades and to Rick Campbell, who has been director of the Press for the past decade — the most productive ten years in Anhinga's history.

> — *Donald Caswell*
> *January 2004*
> *Kansas City, Kansas*

I make the books. I like to imagine the poets that I design and edit for, opening their first box of books and smiling — for we have made a beautiful book, a book that pleases us both.

Making books is a collaboration for me. I hope the way we do it at Anhinga is a process that empowers the poet; that our collaboration has "birthed" a physical object that honors their work and honors the readers that will come later. There's something about a poem on a well designed page — it is somehow better, just as a poem read well aloud is a more enjoyable, coherent experience than one mumbled in a dark smoky room. I try to present poems so the page has motion and carries the reader along. The poet and I sometimes spend a month just choosing a font that we both feel fits the work. This is a luxury that a larger press might not find practical, but when the book is shipped, we are all much happier.

I must admit, I did not map out this process when I started designing books for Anhinga — it evolved. The first prize winner I worked with sent an e-mail about his friend who was depressed for a year after his first book was published because the cover — a shocking cartoonish melange of purple and orange — was both unexpected and totally at odds with the tenor of the book. This was a cautionary tale for me, and the beginning of a growing empathy for the poets I work with.

Collaboration is a curious process. The poet and I are both invested in how the book will look. We want the best result — a beautiful book — but we don't always know what that will be at the beginning. On our path through fonts, page layouts, covers, and corrections, we both come to know the book and each other better. I am grateful for the opportunity to know so many literate, passionate writers. While receiving a book shipment is usually a cause for rejoicing for everyone, it can also be a let down, for I know that the poet and I will not be working together as closely again (until, perhaps the next book).

It is all about the words and being able to hold them in your hands.

— *C. L. (Lynne) Knight*
January 2004
Tallahassee, Florida

In the cold rain today I was thinking about this anthology, how sometimes it seemed to take as long to do as Anhinga's thirty year tenure. I thought of Crosby, Stills, & Nash at Woodstock, "Three days man. Three days. We just love you. We just love you." It's been a long job.

CSN went on to say "tell them who we are. They'll know if we just sing." I suppose those words too are appropriate to where we find ourselves today.

Thirty years ago when Van Brock and his compatriots were bringing out their first Anhinga books, I was probably on an interstate ramp somewhere, maybe that one in Barstow where I was the seventeenth hitchhiker in a queue twenty people deep. I was trying to get a ride east, anywhere east. When all of this began, I confess to being nowhere around. I didn't know anything about publishing poetry or poetry itself.

Now, thirty years later, it's become in large part what I do. In the last few years, I've been praised some for my efforts at Anhinga, and I appreciate that praise, but I want to take this space and time to praise and thank others. First, Lynne Knight, who edits and designs our books. Without beautiful books, a press is nothing. And, the many many poets we have worked with — all of them have been patient and generous. I have to thank my wife Marcia, too. She puts up with my complaining about having too much to do, and she cooks magnificent meals when poets and friends come to our house. I need to thank my daughter Della as well, who thinks I travel too much when I ought to be home all the time just being her daddy.

Thirty years — from the first chapbooks of Donald Caswell, Hal Shows, Sam Harrison, and David Kirby, from the first full-length book by Michael Mott, through twenty Anhinga Prize winners, and collections by such noted poets as Robert Dana, Lola Haskins, and Naomi Shihab Nye — this has been a good long ride.

What are we proud of? Survival, yes. But much more. We're proud that Anhinga Prize winners such as Judith Kitchen, Jean Monahan, Janet Holmes, Frank X. Gaspar, Ruth Schwartz and others have gone on to publish with other presses and win other prizes. We are proud that all of our Anhinga poets have won so many prizes and honors.

Proud that Patti White's poem "Tackle Box," from her prize winning book of the same name, has been made into a prize winning short film and is being shown at the Sundance Film Festival. We're proud that poets who've published with other larger presses, thought Anhinga Press was worthy of their poems. Most of all we are proud that poets published by Anhinga Press like us and feel that we have treated them well. Since we are not going to get rich doing this, we are glad that we are liked and our efforts appreciated. We do our best.

As we move through this thirtieth year and look forward to the future, what do we want? More of the same, I guess. More good books. More good poets. It's good work if you can get it. If it's true, as Williams said in "Asphodel, That Greeny Flower," that —

> *It is difficult*
> *to get the news from poems*
> *yet men die miserably every day*
> *for lack*
> *of what's found there.*

— then we are doing our part in the the great struggle. Thirty years man, thirty years. We just love this. We just love this. This is who we are.

— *Rick Campbell*
Sycamore, Florida
January 2004

1 Anhinga originally was in the umbrella of the Apalachee Poetry Center, which I began at Florida State University to apply for grants and sponsor readings and other projects. The funds and proceeds were kept in the non-profit Florida State University Foundation until Anhinga Press was later incorporated as a non-profit in Florida by Tallahassee attorney and poet Steve Huss.

2 "And Anhinga, the Bird, fabled water-turkey whose existence is no fable, whose presence is my delight, my rapture of living — it is enough for me that he lives. To which page of prodigies again, on what tables of russet waters and white rosettes, in the golden room of the great saurians, will he affix tonight the absurd paraph of his neck?" — *Saint-John Perse*

3 *Café at St. Marks.* The San Marcos Spanish mission, fort, and museum are just south of Tallahassee.

4 *The Space Behind the Clock.* The title, from *Alice in Wonderland,* was the title of one of the poems.

5 Donald Caswell, *Watching the Sun Go Down;* Sam Harrison, *Okra;* Hal Steven Shows, *A Breath for Nothing;* David Kirby, *The Opera Lover.*

6 Valerie Chronis Bickett, *Valerie;* Mary Ann Coleman, *Disappearances;* Francis Poole, *Gestures;* Fabian Worsham, *The Green Kangaroo;* and later still Rick Lott, *Digging for Shark Teeth;* and Leon Stokesbury, *The Royal Nonesuch.*

7 I spent part of one summer at the Hambidge Center for the Creative Arts, at Rabun Gap, Georgia, where Michael and his family were in residence and lived in a mountain cabin surrounded by wild grasses. His wife Margaret was a master weaver teaching weaving classes there — where weaving had been a tradition and there were many large looms. Margaret wove a fabric used to bind a

hard cover special edition of 100 signed copies, which paid for the publication. Michael later was chosen by the Merton Trust to do the official critical biography of Thomas Merton, for which he received a Guggenheim Fellowship. *The Seven Mountains of Thomas Merton,* issued in the U.S. and England, was for a while a best-seller.

8   In 1997, Rick Campbell resurrected the Florida series — issuing full-length books now instead of chapbooks.

ANHINGA PRESS BOARD OF DIRECTORS

2004

C. L. (Lynne) Knight
President

Stephanie Sgouros
Treasurer

Melanie Rawls-Abrams
Secretary

John Simpson
Web Master

Valerie Anthony

Russell Franklin

Joann Gardner

Steven Seliger

Rick Campbell
Director

SNAKEBIRD

THIRTY YEARS OF ANHINGA POETS

ORIENT

Nick Bozanic

Waking early, before the others begin
to remove the traces of sleep from their eyes,
I carry the map etched in my palm into the light.

A warm wind with rain approaches out of the south.
The sagging barn breathes deep in its bones.
The lumbering willows stretch and yawn,
as three ducks stagger across the lawn
to the river rumoring among hunchbacked stones.
In the house behind me, under a loam of wool
our children open like seeds toward the sun.

Facing east I raise my open hand to read
in this nest of lines the course I hold:

You are here. You are here.

Nick Bozanic

1   Up on the roof all afternoon,
replacing broken shingles,
humming through tight lips and nailheads
Rejoice, Rejoice, Immanuel,
I watch my daughter run
spreadeagle-armed
in a circle of light.

Over Hinckley's barn, a hawk,
like her shadow against the sky,
follows in the pattern of the dance.

2   The high sun makes everything heat.
The tarry shingles blacken my hands and knees.
My head swims; for a moment
the crown of the nearest willow
is a pool of flowing leaves
into which I could dive, birdlike,
and be swallowed in the fragrant shadows.

Nick Bozanic

Beyond the screen of autumn trees, wild geese cross
a monstrance sun, while, nearer, wind-spun leaves dance
bright as votive candle flames; the dusk-dimmed moon's an angel
ascending *ad altare Dei* — as Isaac once in ceremony
climbed beside his father Mt. Moriah, sticks on his back for burning
himself to death upon: unconscionable sacrifice

Abraham's God devised to divine what sacrifice
we would *not* make, what affront not tolerate, what cross
not bear. And to His horror He found none: burning
with base desire to please Him, we would unceremoni-
ously annihilate whatever we imagined He demanded, then dance
like David naked before His Ark. Therefore, the seventh angel

of the Apocalypse, the holocaustal angel,
will be all forsaken sons and daughters burning
as one in the perfected night of our destruction, a dance
of light against unfathomable darkness, and lustral ceremony
of longed-for fulfillment: the sacrifice at last of Sacrifice
and consummation of Golgotha's Cross.

As if in procession, wind-rent clouds now cross
where before the wild geese flew: another sort of ceremony,
this passing, and the seasons in their circling dance
describing, finally, the all-embracing O — Omega, angel
of oblivion. Tomorrow our neighbors will gather for sacrifice
the fallen leaves, mound them into tumuli and set them burning,

their black smoke briefly blotting out a sun itself burning
steadily down to darkness. Is this, is every dying, then, a sacrifice?
And do we, dying, give back light? And does our light, if any, cross
the desert spaces between hearts, as sunlight, like an angel
of annunciation heralding the daily ceremony
of dawn, awakens us again to dance?

For life is, after all, more like a dance
than a forced march toward some destination, a ceremony
measured by and measuring time, not distances. We sacrifice
progress for the privilege of merely being here, of burning
ourselves to ash on earth, just as the still-ascending angel
moon above consumes herself in the heavens she moves across

in her own slow dance among those stars like candles burning
in the hands of other angels, acolytes illumining this ceremony
of solitude and self-sacrifice, which is our world and one true cross.

PEARS, WALNUTS, AND A GLASS OF WINE

Nick Bozanic

— after a painting by Chardin

The garden darkens steadily
through every shade of patience.
The spade hangs on its peg

in the tool shed, gloves
on a bench, boots
on the flagstone floor.

The rain goes on falling,
and the eavestroughs mimic
the speech of streams.

On the unattended altar — a kitchen
table at twilight —
the tumbler of wine, broken walnuts,

three pears (the green of vigils),
and an ebony-handled knife
offer themselves openly to an absence

that is everywhere, and near.
The evening deepens. The silence
is a garden darkening in the rain.

The pears, the walnuts, the wine —
the unsolicited gift of Being's gifts —
wait for nothing, there, where nothing other is.

Nick Bozanic

Gem-bodied bees.
Fleabane, catch-fly, phlox.

Chipmunk's chip, chip, chip, chip,
chip, chip, chip, chip, chip, chip, chip.

Grosbeak, goldfinch, redstart, sparrow.
Monarch, viceroy, swallowtail, admiral.

Sunlight, wind. Sunlight, calm.
Sunlight, starlight, moonlight, dawn.

Swift, swift, swift, swift, swift, swift, swift.

Nick Bozanic

Less than half a very dark blue crayon, its paper sleeve torn
and hollow, the wax stub blunt as a bullet, lies on the carpet.
I should pick it up, put it away, or toss it. My son, Gabriel,
is playing over there by the bookcases; he has my watch
in hand and is shaking it and crooning; his eyes smile.
It is morning. Someone on the radio says something dreadful
has happened somewhere, but I'm not really listening.
I am watching Gabriel shake my Seiko to make its bracelet
rattle softly. I sip coffee from a mug. My wife makes sandwiches
in the kitchen. I hear her measured movements,
the muffled murmur of drawers opened and closed, of a knife
cutting bread. I pick up the bit of crayon and put it on the shelf
well above Gabriel's head. He looks at me and drops the watch.
I put my hands under his arms and lift him and kiss his brow
and set him down again. Sunlight as palpable as the wind
from an explosion moves through the room. Gabriel
is walking wobbily toward the kitchen. His mother says,
"Sweetheart." That's all. You understand. *All.*

Nick Bozanic

Marbles in a sack — cat's eyes, aggies, steel
ball-bearings bright as ice in the after-lunch light of high summer;

that great rock back of the school-house we hacked at with our hammers,
hunting for fossils in the folds of slate, and, finding them, feeling
with filthy blistered fingertips the remnant ridges of leaf and scale,
our voices soft as subterranean rain
kissing the mineral density of their names —
trilobyte, brachiopod, cephalapod, lingula;

the squirm of salamanders — orange efts succulent as soft sweets,
(in ponds they were newts and green,
like legged trout with red flecks measled),
the fat night-blue black ones with their sulfurous yellow polka dots,
the sinister red-stripes — we clawed up with bits of bark
and leaf mold from beneath stone and deadfall,
our cupped hands held to eager eyes, those tiny toes
scrabbling for a hold on furrowed palm-flesh;

and for the throwing there were stones, of course, stones, naturally,
and sticks, crab apples, green cherries, berries, too,
(the raspberry's tiny skep, the coarser black-
berry's nubby cap — the both like myriad-faceted bug-eyes —
and the nobly indelible blue blood of the blueberry);
eggs, when we could snatch them from under hens in coops
or from nests in tree or shrub or beneath the eaves
or in attics where the pigeons roosted among the broken lathes; yes,
and always the dried grass-shaft javelins heaved with all our hearts
at each other's heads or anything upright,
post or person, poor birds perched on wires (preferably barbed),
passing cats or kid sisters, barn doors, and best of all the cob-
webbed panes of thin glass high in the holey walls of forsaken houses;
and when nothing else offered, we flung garnet-studded granites
from the railroad bed at the bright bull's eye of the sun;

we scooped water out of ponds and puddles,
out of the barrel beneath the eavespout
where larval insects fidgeted under the scum we skimmed
off and finger-flicked into each other's faces;

frog spawn we grabbed up in great dripping gobs
and kept in Mason jars until the polliwogs wiggled out.

What else? What more? What *not*? Oh,

keys and coins, door knobs and drawer pulls, a dog's paw,
the faux-horn haft of a hunting knife,
grasshoppers like scraps of burnt paper,
the cobbled flesh of mottled toads like pockets of mud,
the red-eared slider's scalloped shell, slender head, and leathery legs,
a fly caught with one quick sweep and clutch of the hand
over the rough-grained wood windowsill where the paint had peeled. ...

In memory, that felt recall of all our long-gone here-and-nows,
what matters is what matter *is:* the palpable presence
of the palpable present, the perfect
flawfulness of the unabsolute
                                    held.

WITHIN THE WORLD
IS THE WORLD WITHIN

Nick Bozanic

Waking on a park bench beneath the maple that shades a bridle path,
I walked across the lawns to the open door of a house in which the child
had set a pitcher of milk (so cold and white each glass I drank
seemed a verse in the legends of snow) and a clutch of bananas
(like nesting crescent moons asleep in each other's luminous arcs)
on the table where I placed my hat before I sat at the desk
at the window outside of which a single star looked down
on the boat someone had left adrift on the pond, and I wrote:

> *Like the ghosts of old men's shadows*
> *a host of crows pecks and scratches*
> *at the filthy salt on the frozen road,*
> *their glossy, tattered cloaks clattering*
> *in the cold wind that blows the drifting snows*
> *across distant meadows.*
>
> *First one, then another, then another crow coughs,*
> *Until the whole troupe in chorus roars*
> *like a fire of stone …*

I put down my pen, put on my hat, went out and closed the door.
I paced the lawn as far as the shore, where I found you asleep
with the child, and a bird in the sedges sang:

> *A dream is all it is is all*
> *a dream is all it is. …*

And I woke on a bench by a tree near the house
through the open door of which a child ran
with a glass of milk and a mottled banana
and a paper hat cut like a crown with stenciled stars,
and she said to me, *Can we go for a ride in the boat?*
And I answered, *Yes.* And a bird in the maple sang:

A dream is all it is is all
a dream is all it is....
And I woke at my desk in the room with no door.
The cat had stepped in its saucer of milk
and tracked wet paws across the floor.
A banana peel lay blackened on the coals.
I looked out the window into the night.
One star swam against the grain of light
like a drunken boat above the maple tree.
I put on my hat and went to lie on the bench
in the park so I could look up and up to see
whatever there might be above
to help us find our way below
before we fall asleep.

HATS

Earl S. Braggs

*Hats play an important part in the emotions of men.... The first
thing the freed slaves thought about was a name and the second
was a hat.*
— Booker T. Washington

Felt tip fedoras and fox-fur-trimmed brims, red Paris tams
and deep navy blue berets, Yankee-blue baseballs and orange Orioles,
flattop white sailorboys and dull colored Greek fishermen,
cold corduroy Texas cowboys and khaki green safaris,
sky caps, short nap caps, and caution-light-yellow hard hats,
all going hurriedly in a thousand different ways
looking for a quiet lunch at noon.

Today the moon and the sun occupy the same skyline
I stare into as I sit wearing my father's hat, thinking.
Tonight a stranger will sleep on this very bench and call it home.
All around me little children playing catch in winter coats
and hats remind me of the vividly colored visions of my youth
when it was much colder than it now seems.
I think I will call it the winter of hats.

We found them under Mama's bed. No one said we couldn't
so we did what any boy would do. Tyrone was the first to try one on
and he was a sight to be seen; I mean he looked like an old church
lady with a green bean bowl on top of her head with red feathers
all pointing full speed ahead. Then my younger uncle Richard
and I tried on the one that made us look like Gypsy queens.

It was the winter Mama returned after ten years.
I had just turned seventeen.
She never told us why she left and we never asked.
Maybe we didn't want to know, maybe we did. I can't remember.
Anyway, we had a box full of women's hats of every color.

1969 and we were on a mission and we didn't care
about anything as long as everything fit into our small scheme
of things. We were caught between doing time and listening
to the voice of H. Rap Burn-Baby Brown, watching war
rage on the evening news and hearing riots breaking windows
on the radio station playing the same song over and over
like a broken Billie Holiday. Bless the child bless the child bless.

Then someone would change to James Brown, "I feel good"
and we felt good as we could sliding across the floor
in our too-tight live wire orange pants that didn't match
anything, especially a gold and black checkerboard hat.
We didn't care how we looked as long as we looked crazy.
The ghetto respects crazy people and ex-prisoners.
Everyone knows that.

We were the hat people waiting for the weekend to begin,
standing on Tally's comer wearing a full maxi tweed that didn't need
a thing but a virgin wool scarf to wrap around the cold night
life at the Dew-Not-Drop-Inn unless you are well known
or invited. Drunk and spilling beer into the next morning
classroom blues, "Mr. Braggs, please take your hat off,"
Monday school teacher says.
Perhaps she didn't know that Mama gave us hats
to protect our soft feelings while she made ends meet
that have never met before by selling liquor
in our dollar-shot glass house full of hats.

My father died at the end of that winter. He drank too much
too soon. He was a good dad that lived some other place.
For the funeral, Mama bought us hats like the ones men wore.
As she gave them to us she looked in our eyes and said,
"You can tip them but don't take them off in church;
it's bad luck."

IN WHICH LANGUAGE
DO I KEEP SILENT

Earl S. Braggs

for Cathie

I know that if a number is raised to the 1st power,
the exponent 1 is usually not written.
I know that the absolute value of a number is that number
without its sign. Without a sign, there is no way to tell who I am.
Today I will not give any indications.

I know that the angular velocity of your movement is too
beautiful to name and I've come to recognize you as a dancer
in lines of my own poetry.
It's a funny thing how books can be read upside down and
maps get us most lost. I know this from experience.

Lately, I find myself looking at maps.
measuring distances between cities.
One inch = twenty-five miles. 1/25 of one inch = 1 mile
Small towns are represented as dots. I question
the mathematics of it all.
My whole numbers have become fractions on a November calendar
I've learned to count parts of each square. I know
what it's like to have nothing but time.

The night I first saw you dance, I followed the softness
of your steps across the floor, across the studio, every spin taken
into consideration, every jump. I know the shortest distance
between us is a straight line. I want to leap
with you but not tonight because when I divide the time of day
into the time I've known you
multiplied by the number of times you've crossed my mind
lately, the answer is way too early to tell what I'm feeling.
I know the wrong answer is not always wrong.

Do you know how to tango? Would you teach me to ride music
in wide open space? Would you teach me to dance
to the unexplained, deliberate as the unexplored dances
to the patterns of treasure maps? Would you teach me
to close my eyes when I kiss?

I know that the co-efficient of A to the second power is 1.
I know what it feels like to be alone in a room too many nights
in a row. I know how to fly without wings.
If you were a jet airplane traveling at 7.50 km while
gaining altitude at a constant rate, if you traveled between points
5.80 km apart, what is the gain in altitude? I would figure it out
and meet you at the vertex. I know the Pythagorean Theorem.

I know that some mornings my dreams lie to make me feel better.
I laugh, trying to figure the ones I now have. I'm not saying I dream
about you. I'm saying you are in my dreams and most often I wake up
falling. I know the distance I fall = 1/2 times the acceleration
times the time squared it takes me to fall.

According to maps, my silence is one mile away from you
in either direction. I know that speed = distance
divided by the time I sit here and wait.
I know exactly how long it should take if I were to measure your gaze
in either of the two languages I now speak.

I light myself another cigarette. I don't say a thing.
I ponder the velocity of silence.

JUST ANOTHER BUS STATION BOY

Earl S. Braggs

It's July. It's hot and many are without
shirts or sleeves long enough
to cover tattooed dragons and snakes
clawing down arms

that have been singed one time too many to feel
the heat of being afraid of what
the next town is sure to bring. Jimmy Lea sings

his way along the suitcase aisles
of this transit lifestyle while he smokes
what's left of an empty pack of Viceroys
dangling from the mouth of this small town boy

looking for a big time in a big city full
of lights and night time ladies strolling avenues
in night time dresses too short to remember

how many times Jimmy and his guitar have walked
into pawn shops and shopped 'til
only Jimmy Lea walked out

into the street of summertime heat, thinking
he never knew his daughter's name
just as his father never knew his
way was the only way for a black boy and his guitar in 1969

when a war was in every envelope, waiting
to be ripped open. But Jimmy Lea doesn't plan
to be home when the mailman comes
walking up onto that front porch that looks like his mother,
rundown, but still standing.

He looks around every Route 40 town and he sees
the same, the same mama in red hot-pants dragging

the same half dressed son to the restroom and the same father
with a pencil thin moustache running from the law,
the same hobos and gigolos and you-knows
selling oregano grass marijuana at the cab stand

across the street, the same ticket takers
dressed in hound dog grey, punching holes through destinations,
the same group of homeboys carrying shoeshine boxes and rags
trying to steal luggage and bus station locker keys

cut a little bit too flat to open the door for Jimmy Lea.
So it's one more night of not having a soft Greyhound seat
to sleep from Oklahoma City to Salt Lake.

Tonight he will go to the side of town
where the train station lives and have a soul food dinner,
some good ole collard greens full of ham hocks.

Tomorrow he will buy a shoe box and a bunch-a-rags
with his last 8 dollars, walk back to the bus station
and see if he can shine a nice glow
on a pair of Mr. Norton's Stacy Adams.

AND THIS IS SPRING IN RUSSIA

Earl S. Braggs

Birch trees come alive, groves at a time.
Two weeks ago it snowed, covered all of the East
and stopped exactly at the line, the sign,
Russia.

I crossed the bleak border at night. My wife
beside me in the back seat of a German grey car.
All the passports and visas in the world were not enough
to explain my choice of borders to cross. We entered
from Poland.

Every piece of luggage was unpacked, unpacked and
unpacked and not repacked by the searchers
of small mistakes in small print. They could not

find any wrinkles in my dark face not accounted for.
Still they, the searchers of small mistakes,
kept us waiting for, it seems, hours of small questions
that repeated themselves until the questioners became
the questions. Finally

with great hesitation the road leading to where
we were going was, of course, narrow and blacker
than any American night I remember. Some say
this road with trees on either side covered any sign
of German convoy movement between war year first
and war year last.

We drove on to the sound of death rumbling
in the branches of birch trees. No light,
except occasional headlights and even they
were somehow more frightening on dark narrow roads
when one knows the history of such scenes.

My wife leaned in to comfort me. I repacked the scatteredness
of my mind. Behind us, the road disappeared
into the promise of morning spring showers and the smell
of kindly planted flowers.

Earl S. Braggs

For Anastasiya

And yet on these rare occasions
the magic secret of magic moments is sometimes revealed
by the way the sun rises the morning after
a night of winter rain. I did not

know it then. I was laughing, not quite enjoying
myself stranded yellow in a corner chair
in a room of too many conversations. Everything empty
until she arrived. Your mother

was wearing a winter red St. Petersburg overcoat.
I was wearing construction boots. I was rebuilding my life.
I did not have enough parts to finish
the smallest of hovering small talk that seemed
to exclude and include the nothingness

until she strolled into the light. So unassumingly beautiful
no rain had fallen upon the shoulders of her coat.
The room divided into quad-quiet angles before resuming
its stagnant pose. The air was thick with promise

and though stars were not visible, I knew the dipper
had positioned itself directly above me for the evening.
Slowly as she moved around the room, my rhyme became
the rhythm of winter rain.

Her eyes found me, yet I could not leave
my yellow chair. My construction boots saw the parts
that had gone so many years missing, yet they, too,
refused to unlace in the face of promise. Like me

they, too, had been broken too many times to trust
winter rain love. That night I knew
there's no gold at the end of the rainbow. I knew
vanity has never been fair. And I knew

love at first sight is a tired, worn out, hungry phrase
but that night it felt right and it proved appropriate
the morning after our first winter rain.

So my dear Anastasiya, three years after the morning after
you took your first steps in Russia, your mother
still wears her St. Petersburg red overcoat and my boots
have long been discarded. I don't need them now.

I found the angles to build my room
in your mother's eyes that winter night of rain.

STRIPPED BY THE LIGHTS
(LAS VEGAS, NEVADA)

Earl S. Braggs

A rustling Vegas wind cuts across miles
of sagebrush and vanes, the lure of whirling wheels,
opulent showrooms, and easy money magic.

Rattle the "bones," then sigh is the only sound
in town. Death Valley is on Las Vegas Boulevard. I stand

and watch penniless families leave the way they came,
Interstate 15. Stripped by the lights on the strip.

Neoned and tinseled on Paradise Road, the other way
they now go blackjack, bingo, poker, roulette, and Keno.
The casino never closes

its eyes. By the time they reach Red Rock thirteen miles away,
they'll be ready to come back and play slot machines

in every restaurant, drugstore, supermarket and laundromat.
Not enough quarters to wash their clothes before they left
Las Vegas. Now

the strip is stripping her dirty clothes slow as they go
in a broadway burlesque and magic show. The odds

ultimately favor the "House." Death Valley
is on Las Vegas Boulevard.

But just as many families come to face the lure
of whirling wheels

turning hundred dollar bills into brown shiny pennies.
Even I, with nothing to lose, lost my faith
in the red turn of rocks. This desert town loves

only Sammy Davis, Jr., and Sinatra
is still singing at the MGM Grand Hotel and the Battle
of the Buccaneer is still re-enacted every ninety minutes.
Another family leaves with nothing

but brown shiny pennies. Another family will find out
how dark a desert night drive can be. But this city

where Flashlight is a small plaza next to a theatre
will cast the glow back to oasis with Royal Flush
intentions and win. The odds

ultimately favor the "House." Illusion and her sister,
Fantasy, are mirages on Sahara Desert Avenue.
This is my advice to you

young man with beautiful wife and three glamorous daughters,
"Bring enough clothes so you don't have to use
the laundromat in Las Vegas." This is not Walt

Disney World. This is the lure of the whirl. Vegas
is a red rock girl and Caesars is a palace, 1,509
suites of luxury with No Smoking rooms available on request.

James Brock

My child, in his room, is playing,
and I cannot tell whether he
is laughing or crying, but I will
not stir from my reading, for his joy,

as I imagine, over the leaves
of sycamore we found is his own,
and if his noise is the child's
grief, that, too, is his own. To be

truthful, I am afraid that I can
no longer restore comfort out of pain.
Still, I know I will seek in the broad
ways whom my soul loves, and I

retrieve one trick I learned young,
so that I do rise and go. I mix
sugar milk and take paper and matches
into his room. *Here,* I tell him,

I have something to show you. With
the liquid, he traces circles
with his finger upon the paper, and I
lay my hand over his hand, to feel

the movement of what he has in mind.
The circles, I think, become smoother,
rounder, smaller. I say, *Okay,*
let's let the paper dry, and

I return to my reading, and he
to his quieter play. And it is fear
again: how a father dreams of
the drowning child he can never save,

the child's face disappearing
in a swallow of silt, how a father
plays with combustible materials
and their traces — fire and ash — that

will leave nothing but the child's
tiny bones. It is fear because I know
my son will come to me, asking
if it is ready, and I will have

to say yes. I will light the match
beneath the paper, and from nothing
will appear maybe something like a face,
something like my own face,

fevered, blistered, blackening faster
than the paper, or the design becomes
my child's face in a cry or a laugh,
calling out someone else's name.

TO THE CORONER WHO DID NOT HAVE TO DRAW MY BLOOD

James Brock

sixteen years ago, and centrifuge
the alkaline hydrocarbons from my blood,
contributing to the Ada County records
another fact concerning how much gasoline
is too much for the teenaged male
to ingest, who did not have to split
me open, to remove what remained
of the liver, or to cut the lung tissue
to recover the amount of fluid that bled
through the membrane, who did not have
to decide between suffocation or poisoning,
all the while I was pounding the door
of God's speakeasy, having arrived without
the password for the two eyes that hid
behind the door slit and that rolled *oh
brother* when I guessed "Rimbaud's three-legged
cat," and the eyes' voice said, "Get lost,
kid," so I left thinking what a piss-ant
job for an angel, coming back to the world,
my parents' garage, puking something blue
and thin onto the pavement, I give my thanks
to you, as I know you would have been
tender for this late adolescent, whose torso
had just lengthened to man-size, whose
hands were strengthening, whose skin
stretched young and fluid, for you
would have whispered, "Goddamn it,"
with the incision, remembering your own
son, or yourself, and I give you
thanks, for I may be the one you
blessed when you once cursed over
that old man's drink, a Manhattan, "If there
would be one suicide who didn't come

my way," and I tell you now it was me
who didn't come your way, cold, blue,
youthful, rotted, who today rose
with his beloved from the Modoc Lava Caves,
whose bearings were lost in the desert
afternoon light haloing silver off
automobiles and asphalt and ash.

LOVER'S KEY, FLORIDA

James Brock

> And a man in love, besides, is always fearful.
> So I decided to give myself a reason
> To have a grievance.
> — *Ovid*

Easy arrivals, Ovid, old friend,
my grievance is with them. The tide
will soon out, and the water will
recede and leave the destitute clutter
my lover and I will rummage
and recast. How old are these shells,
these dolphin bones, still white?
Recent, I must think. At this beach,
the gulf's modest economies
relinquish their capital: sea grass,
urchins, sibilant matter. The gulf,
you would think, has in it a voice
— a pain — that covers everything.

Only the sound itself is everything:
a Caspian Tern chitting, or de Leon's
Spanish marking, or today, an
American sighing, "This is nice.
This is some beach." Sounding
insists on repetition. How else are we
to be fixed, if not by echolocation?

My beloved covers her skin with sun
block, draws out a towel, sits,
and enjoys herself — it's an ocean,
not a waterfall, after all. She turns
to me. "Need some? It's Florida,
you know," and she points
to the sun, which touches and burns

everything white, so that it becomes
necessary for me to remember
snow, an Idaho snow that once
could cover everything, quiet
everything in my childhood.

"Sure," I tell her, "I'll take some."
While I am grateful, I sometimes wish
to lie in snow, which also bleaches
and preserves the body, if it is
a dry snow, if it stays cold
enough long enough.

THE BOUGAINVILLEA,
YOUR BLACK DRESS

James Brock

After all, the sky flashes, the great sea yearns,
we ourselves flash and yearn ...
— *John Berryman*

After the detonate wind, after the hurricane
            three years ago, you saved the bougainvillea,
                        sheering the broken limbs, untangling
the knotted veins for more light. You told me

how the leaves, ankle-deep, were papery,
            clean, like the discarded wings of insects.
                        For two days, your hands were swollen,
for the thick, tumorous net of thorns pierced

through the layers of your gloves. Surely,
            I think, your lover then held your hands,
                        coveting those wounds he could
tend, and he nearly wept as he salved

your palms. The beauty is in the bougainvillea's
            deformity, its danger, you said. Today, I
                        asked for this, all of this, over the phone,
while on your line harps played on the radio,

either Debussy or Ravel or Faurè, we could
            not name. The music sounded like a Degas
                        woman shadowed by candle, or you
in your black dress, before the bougainvillea,

a sea of outrageous coral, too full and
            swollen, a renovation of sex and
                        abundance, a swirling of a hunger
you could live by. When you say touch does not

make beauty repulsive, you are right.
        Love, all my life, my body has been
                impatient, ambient only with want.
When you wear your black dress — the seam

that splits at your breasts, the extravagance
        of your skin and hair — I see a woman
                dressed in the last sensible idea,
a happiness distinct from melancholy. Yes,

beauty is not an island, but a siren,
        scorching the sky with flash and
                yearn, and we ourselves are flashing
and yearning. And if we lose a little blood

on a twist of thorns? And if we become
        a little infected? When you wear your
                black dress, I will come to you,
ungloved.

James Brock

First, *my* backyard, the Cuban laurel
tree, neither Cuban nor laurel, would be
a good start, but with its
leaf and creeper, it keeps the St. Augustine
grass at bay. So I am left to contemplate
the killing of the other exotics, the available
snake plants, those variegated swords with
tendrilled tubers, and thus I have begun to go
native in Florida. Sure, I have
thinned the ligustrums and shell-ginger lily,
sheared the croton, but I am still learning
the names of exotics: you, carrotwood, you corn
plant, you bird of paradise and
jacaranda, you bougainvillea, frangipani,
banana, Hong Kong orchid tree, you
umbrella plant and Mexican heather, you Surinam
cherry and Valencia orange, and you
weeping bottlebrush and you whatever,
all of you an Ohioed dream of Florida, so much backdrop
for *The Creature from the Black Lagoon*, I say
must go. But who would
not want that kind of 3-D Florida
in 1954, to be startled
by it, after a hard day of filming, even if it's just
a B-movie, to be Ben Chapman, spending six
hours latexed in a modified diving suit, half
an alligator boy's body from the roadside
attraction and the rest a Chinatown fish-dragon's
head, carrying around slinky Julia Adams all day,
and finally unzipping the gill-man's mask,
freeing his head to the subtropic air
and light? Of course, what Ben Chapman
wants first is a good smoke, then a high-ball,
and the next day a round of golf, a trip

to Palm Beach for a quick fuck, and he
thinks he could very well live here, forget
Pasadena and snap up that tiny
bungalow in Sanibel, grow mangoes and oranges
and Brazilian pepper, and go fishing
out in the Gulf of Mexico.
What might he leave after he goes? A Florida worth a little
killing? Today, I believe my neighbor's bishofia
might be an even better start,
save for that downy woodpecker, behind me, holed up
in the dead arm of the Cuban laurel tree,
that
one-ounced brute, eyeing me.

UPON HEARING THAT MY GRANT APPLICATION WAS PASSED OVER AND THE WINNER WAS A BIO-TECH PROFESSOR WHO HAS DESIGNED GENETICALLY-ALTERED PROTEIN FOR BUCKWHEAT SEED

James Brock

— for Denise Duhamel

Okay, call me Sylvia Plath. I wanted that award,
the crystal glass eagle, the pendant, the certificate,
the lapel pin, the thousand bucks, and the parking space
next to the university president's spot—the whole
platinum and sapphire tiara. I knew I should have
written that poem on the manipulations
of amino acid balance in buckwheat seed proteins.
I knew I should have named that new genetic
strand *Omicron-Brockide-32,* should have brokered
the patent rights to Monsanto, let them spread the seed
of my pumped-up, high-octane, drought-tolerant,
American-can-do-know-how buckwheat
to sub-Saharan Africa and southern Mongolia.

One year later, then, I would have written
the grant report, presented it to the committee
on PowerPoint, and finished off my presentation
with a streaming video clip, showing some adolescent
boy, from Gambia, say, and he would be eating
my buckwheat flat bread, and there he would be,
digitalized, smiling, full and muscular. Yes,
and at that moment, vindicated and wise,
teary-eyed and generous, the grant committee
would gather and lift me on their shoulders, laughing
and singing, joyful for all the corporate sponsorships that

would follow me and bless our humble home
institution. For me, dare I dream further confirmations?
O, to be Nationally Endowed, Guggenheimed, Nobelled!

Of course, in Gambia, and other geographies
beneath the sweep and hoozah of fellowships
and announcements in *The Chronicle of Higher Education,*
the newly nourished could be striking the flint
of their first syllables of their first poems, poems
whose phrases — under the most subdued of flames — would
coolly scorch and burn our best American intention.

CHAGALL AMONG DEVELOPERS

Van K. Brock

He will spend his last days on a hill below,
near St.-Paul-de-Vence. Now, here, above Vence,
agents hound him for his view, his home,
where he works. On clear days, the Mediterranean
stretching one horizon and the Alps the other,
he inhabits the distances in this bright canvas.
Below, among galleries, villas, puzzled tourists,
posters emerge from the city walls at night
like stains stucco and earthen slips will never
really cover. These worry Algerians, citizens
as well as subjects, now, who often disappear.
Still, the agents dog him to their terms, build
tall villas around him, to wall him in and out.

He's the foreign one if they cannot imagine
his reeling brain needing this sky to house
gaunt forms he restored to laughing health,
many living only through him. If the agents
saw his Jerusalem glass abstractions — deep red
patches bleeding on a blue sky, orange sun
and yellow stars over an earth still green —
the language would certainly elude them.

But his bright oils prove how Provencal air
nurtures villages and fields from elsewhere.
Had one tried to explain how Chagall dissolves
time and gravity to give other realms in us
freer play, as he shows us everything, almost
clairvoyantly, like an impish Ariel swirling
pure pigments on a fluid surface, raising
necessary worlds where goats and cows graze
on flowers among clouds, naturally weightless

barns, synagogues, homes no longer there,
families and villages feasting at weddings
and mitzvahs, deliriously at ease, dancing
in this air again around rituals of innocence
from which they were spun, finally free, now,
of their heavy lives. You see?
They only shrug. *Realty is realty.*

Van K. Brock

He hangs from a gibbet
The red sun
wears a black ring.
Man is a wolf to man.

"I believe in suffering.
It is not feigned in me.
This is my only merit.
I was not made to be so terrible."

The society lady fancies she has a
reserved seat in heaven. Who does
not paint himself a face? We are
insane. We think ourselves kings.
Are we not all convicts?

The Chinese invented gunpowder,
they say, and made us a gift
of it. In all things tears.
War which all mothers hate. This
will be the last time, little father.

"I underwent then a moral crisis
I began to paint with an outrageous lyricism
It was an inner necessity."

For in turning toward his own inwardness
he may become divided from things.

The red sun always
wears a black ring.

THE HINDENBERG

Van K. Brock

*This early showpiece of the Thousand Year Reich
used 850,000 skins of cattle for hydrogen bags.*

It is said that the night it burned
the thunder of panicking hooves
drowned the screams of passengers.

As far away as the buttes of Asia,
one old Siberian woman says that merely
the echo of their lowing still stirs
immense winds and whirlwinds.
                              All the small
meadows of Europe remember their grazing;
cattle-cars and railway platforms shudder
still at their foreshadowings.
                              Untold cobblers
recall the million seams glued and stitched
on screaming machines before their pockets
held enough hydrogen to kindle a conflagration.

The war on nature begun,
eventually, every country in Europe
and many in Africa and Asia were gutted:
in bombings, in battle, at sea, and in the fires,
filth, and hunger of virulent slave pens:
the outward rendering of ageless accumulations
sucked up from the cities and villages of earth,
and the ruins run in and out of us all,
stretching before and behind
for far more than a Thousand Years.

BUCHENWALD

Van K. Brock

Her hands join hands of screams that tear out hair
to wreathe her neck with knowledge. The surgery
of those whose shirt she wears has sheared her.

Is it you, Anna, shirtfront a ravine,
pants around knees? Are you so soon a saint?
I'll lay my body, weeping, by your wrecked house,
as once I marvelled, pierced by your firm vows
never to believe in evil or ever recant.

From this ravaged wood pure flames will leap.

She grins, holds hands with the invisible dead,
beckons, salutes with both hands, wrists
like rubber, tries to shake hair from her fingers,
then smiles again, her womb a falcon's nest,
an Aryan doctor's last ingenious experiment.

Van K. Brock

In the factory of teeth,
ashes fall like snow.
Afterwards, snowflakes,
like little ashen people
cut out of membranes,
dance on soft winds.
But spring can't melt the ash
and the wind blows it away
only to bring it back in
a tangle of ribbons and hair
around a blank face painted
on a child's broken rattle.
These eyes are scissors,
these ashes seeds
the ground labors to absorb.
The white flag struggling
from the branch opens wilted
and slowly straightens its
creases. Sidewise, a small
body dances out. Hymen, O
Hymen, the scissors bleeding.
Look! Its veins are skeletons,
and every leaf's mouth
stitched shut.

Van K. Brock

She and the parents escaped, but she still whispers
to herself: Don't think.
                    Karlsruhe was different
from the north, she said, the people lovelier, gentler.
She always smiles, her eyes vibrant and fervent.

Her two boyfriends were picked up by the state.

Now, with no shelter while incomings explode always,
she knows what those who stayed behind learned
about survival and daily freezing and burning.

From a ravenous cavity, the voices of rasping tongues
push her back, always, saying. Live! Tell!

She wakes with a worried smile, flushed and pale,
everything, all, as weightless as compressed air.

"There's a monster in my sleep doesn't want its name
known. It's bad," she says, simply, smiling, "evil."

CHRIST IN THE SUN

Van K. Brock

(A Spanish padre is sick with fever in the New World.)

Since in our great forests we have no roads
Nor cities, we have dreamed of a land of sun
Merely; though a paradise with neither Christ
Nor a Christian is Satan's work, an illusion of lust
That stirs fantasies as fever stirs my blood
And tempts to conquest, a test for Christian man.

The primitive men we find here are, to us, new men,
Though old world men are also new here. These roads
Bewilder my brain. The vessels of my blood
Are inflamed by the naked savages and their sun.
God tempts us with false freedom; the rank lust
Of old Adam, my enemy, hopes to win me from Christ.

But I will preach them Christ! Christ! Christ!
As the stern fathers did me, from boy to man,
Until I, until they, are stronger than our lust,
Or Christ is stronger in us than these false roads —
And these pagan chants, these dances to the sun,
Like these tempers, are purged from our dark blood.

"O Father, take this darkness from my blood
And brain, make bright for me, in me, Christ's
Pure Light. The simple light of their sun
Must be our darkness. O what is man
That delusion in him can take such subtle roads
He cannot know love from a lie, faith from lust?"

They did receive us freely, despite their lust
For the flesh. Though crude, they have a gentle blood,
A child's pulse for earth and creatures. Their roads

Leave no scars. They have small property. Like Christ
They would rather give than receive. Their shamans
Say they walk in the light of two worlds, two suns.

Yet it is like Eden, this place, with its warm sun,
Its flowers, flesh, fruit, fresh streams. Is it lust
To breathe too deeply, is the faith that cools my blood
Then also false that it can enrage a man
Against such outward grace in the joined names of Christ
And that dreamed life to which death is the one road.

Here, where the one road is the sun's road,
Spain, torn between goldlust and Christ lust,
Drives its two-edged sword into every man's blood.

Van K. Brock

When the missionary died, we stood grouped on the beach,
facing the ocean, out of which he came
singing "Our Father," voices older than speech,
but the waves drowned or beat them back again.

We raised the alien words against the night
for power and magic, for they were strange and vague,
but the sea knew an older chant than that
and night on night it mocked us as we prayed.

Our women, naked, bloomed, half-seen, and drooped.
We ate, but barely tasted the plentiful fruit,
though the trees flowered perennially while we looked
for signs in clouds, meanings in a mute book.

FOURTH OF JULY PARADE, ALBION, WA.

Fleda Brown

Everyone's happy, catching candy.
There's an army truck; one fire truck
screaming; a blue Olds about 1975;
two police cars side by side,
everything huzza-huzza,
the band playing "From the Halls of Montezuma"
from a flatbed truck; eight kids on bikes,
with balloons; a dozen 4-H kids in clover-shirts;
a bulldog with a bow;
two hefty rodeo girls on horses,
a small tractor pulling prizewinning chickens
in their two festooned cages.
I can't help it, I get sentimental tears.
Damn, I say to myself. Chickens.
A prize for being chickens.
Then, amazingly, here they all come again,
back up the street, chickens
from the other side,
fiddle-players instead of horns showing,
candy flying again like stars.
Everything a copy of itself, another chance.
Quantum physics says it's true,
particles coming and going.
The road not taken may be taken.
Meanwhile, the chickens move forward
again in our eyes, the Declaration of Independence
gets signed. We need custom,
return. We like to sit sandal-footed in the grass,
happily surrendered to either side.
Past or future, it's no wonder
the chickens win, the way they keep
their artist's eyes cocked, lost in the work
of being chickens
        again and again.

BUYING THE KING-SIZED BED

Fleda Brown

I'm already thinking of rolling around that expanse,
tossing a leg without entangling. The way I am,

though, I see all the possibilities for loss. I see us
pillowed and billowed, supported in exactly the right

hollows by ergonomically designed, pocketed coils,
while beneath it all — the pea under a royal height —

the oppressed, the downsmashed, sleep in despoiled
cardboard boxes, or three on one frayed blanket.

Think of us, spread out, tongues on the rampage,
marking where we'll kiss. Oh wild God, how can

you permit this excess? How could any of us gauge
the exact distance at which people turn strangers

to each other? In our double bed — called double,
but we have been bumper-cars and cliff hangers

on it for years, our shorter ancestors troubling
us still — I can't even raise my knee

without poking my dear love in the groin.
We have been close, we have understood each other

the way people in tight houses start growing
together — at a molecular level, absorbing

each other's pheromones. Yelling and slamming doors,
too, or else they are lost inside each other! They would

have grand houses, if they could. They would forge
on like jet-skis through the foyer and out to the good

sea. They would send a wire to say, "I still
love you." The sweet old world is longing to be

loose and light. All night long it stares up at the chilled
stars. This is a sticky business, finding the peak

distance for love, knowing our bodies will be nothing,
someday, wanting to hear them make their delicious,

reassuring sounds, bobbing against each other.

Fleda Brown

Fydrich would lift his wild golden curls
and talk to the sky. Hrabosky the same,
and he'd talk to the ball, circling
the mound, face twitching. And then he would
face the centerfield fence, whirl back
around, go into his stretch, and
pitch.
                    It's best not to take chances. You
get your mind stalking and empty.
You slap your glove on your thigh, pace
your pattern. You make a ring of not-caring
around the thing. Too much pressure on one
point and the energy's down a black hole.
Carlton, on the watch for UFOs, what he might
have been doing is picking up an
archipelago as it moved through its
calculations. His mind was just breathing
in and out.
                    So much that's far-fetched
lodges between the in and the out.
Did I mention Luis Tiant, flinging his
head to the sky as his arm came down?
Proof that the center of the world is in
the body, not the sight. You get these actions
together that don't care about each other.
They don't stand for anything.
                                Listen, ball.
Bless you, ball. You and I, ball.
You get into a rhythm. Inside the rhythm
is a pitch. You keep your mind on the
rhythm, waiting to feel the pitch coming on.
You don't know how to speak directly to
the thing you want more than anything.

Fleda Brown

One day Adam said "Adam"
and found out he was standing

across the field from everything
else. It scared him half to death.

He lifted his arms as if they
could help. The air felt cool.

So he said "air" and "cool":
a population of not-Adams

sprouted everywhere. One
of them was Eve, a wild card.

He heard her clearly, distinct
from his internal voice, his

private naming. She was singing
"In time, the Rockies may crumble,

Gibraltar may tumble ..."
and sure enough, it was

something o'clock already.
He saw that her mouth was pink.

"Pink," he said, because it was
small and had lips to push the air

away. And there was something
else, he was sure of it, a softening

of the air between them,
a spell. Nothing could be the word

for it. He was reeling
with the wound of it, the chink

between subject and object.
Light entered, memory followed

and began to tell its own story.
He felt himself held in it,

traveling *within* it, now,
driving toward a particular town.

"Something's happened,"
he said to her, but she'd guessed

the doom of it already, the wooden
signs along the highway

bravely standing for everything
that matters: *Burma Shave,*

*Kollectibles Kottage, The Cock
& Bull.* She ran a finger delicately

along the window as if she could
trace what it was that had

broken loose from the two
of them, that was running crazy

out there, never looking back.

Fleda Brown

An old Candid Camera skit: two men
stop cars at the border. "Delaware's closed
today," they say, and the drivers docilely turn away.

That's me, I'd be still driving around looking.
The way you ought to find a state is, things
change. Fields, then you get to a difference

that stays different, not this compass arc carved
out of Pennsylvania, this right angle drawn away
from Maryland. On a map, its name drifts

in the Atlantic, neither here nor there. It lies
inward like a cove on a creek, twigs and leaves
swirled in, and sludge, and a faint orange ring

you know is pollution, and then in a hard rain
it all moves on and starts again: cancer
slipping boundaries — highest breast cancer rate

in the country, no one takes the blame, everyone's
from somewhere else, like New Jersey, the other side
of the hypotenuse across the bay. In the middle,

Salem Power Plant steams upward, refuses
to take sides. In the south, the long slow marshes,
cypresses, snow geese, herons. Good and evil

cancel each other out — Dela*where?* —
the way the ocean tries to cancel out the shore,
and the shore walks inland and forgets itself in relation

to anything else. I don't know where I live.
You need a breath between states, to be sure
the next one's coming. "Welcome to Oklahoma,

to Missouri, for instance. I remember Arkansas that way,
as being *not those other states*. There have
to be limits, skin and bones. The poetic version

of home can open the mind like a trick-
or-treat bag and endlessly drop things in: Wilmington,
Newark, Middletown, Smyrna, Lewes, Rehoboth,

names our children learn, meaning their own
caches of grief and joy, the resonances
their ears have collected by now. But me, did I

mention I'm starting to lose my hearing? Words
grow softer, doing tricks and transformations.
I could be in a hotel room, soft clicks

in the hallway, a rumble. I can't remember the number
on the door, the sheets are empty pages. I try
to identify the boundaries, as the Buddha says, separate

the strands of experience until there is no self, while
the self is full with the moment, riding the waves
of its own impermanence. I've said farewell, God knows,

many times. The day we left Fayetteville, the three
neighbor children lined up on the sad little mound
of grass to wave goodbye to our son. It was summer,

and the sun took everything out of my eyes
and kept moving. Like a fool, I've believed, though,
in each place. The little creek behind our house

runs clear, now rusty, now clear. Who or what
causes this I do not know. Runoff from lawns,
I'd guess, growing feathery weeds underwater, here,

then gone. Still, there are minnows. And oh yes,
you, my utterly specific love, and our children,
and our children's children, ringing and crashing like deer

to our salt lick, appearing in the morning mist as if
through holes in the universe — their innocence
and light — leaving small berries of scat, and tracks.

READING POETRY AT THE HORSE MEADOW SENIOR CENTER

Fleda Brown

We'd been told fish for lunch, so we took bets on how it would be
cooked and I guess I won, although we couldn't be sure if it was baked
or broiled under the sauce, which, being guests, we pushed around
against the spinach. Not true: some of us ate, including Syd, who lived
nearby and said don't joke, he might *be* here someday, and we were all

scanning tables, seeing our own bodies rounding back to creation, our
exact and precious sufferings slowly leaking out. The beached whale of
poetry, I thought, not seeing Syd but myself, exhausted into prose. Syd
got up, as directed, post-scrod and pre-cobbler, so people wouldn't drift
away, and he read a poem that played up the local, and then I pulled

the mike toward them as far as the cord went, using my old joke about
the end of my rope, and they laughed, and I started with a poem about
my daughter that seemed to end right. Then I read "Dock" because of
its repetition, so they wouldn't miss rhyme too much, that elephant in
the room. I had time between to think of Longfellow, the way

"shining big sea waters" lies off in the varnished distance and leaves a
person free afterward to take a nap. Then I read the one about my
grandfather forgetting where he was and thought halfway through, *uh-
oh*, but they smiled and clapped, sure of where they were, and by this
time those who wanted it had finished a second dish of peach cobbler

and I felt really happy, useful, part of the general flow of things.
I felt like a closing line myself, made of nothing but words intended
to swim out into the stratosphere, but caught, luckily, among the
wheelchairs and walkers.

Fleda Brown

When the polar ice caps melt,
when the water rises at Lewes, this house
with its long porch and white railings,

where we sit in the dark singing "American Pie"
and "Barbara Ann," the verses we remember,
water will slide here under the doors,

will round itself into the cups and bowls,
burrow its veins along the wiring. The pier
where we used to stand, where we walked

the children and admired perch and sand sharks
caught by quiet old men, water will no doubt
hush the lost pilings like the prow

of a sunken ship. On Savannah Road,
the Wicker Picker will turn dazed and drunken
with floating baskets. Those who come after us

will cup their hands, bathe their eyes,
and stare together into the throat of the sea:
"There is where things used to be. No,

maybe there," they'll say. They'll make up
a story of hammers, chain-link fences, trellises,
and desire before the balance shifted.

It will be our story, the porch, the singing,
but broken open, diffuse as salt. They'll taste
the sea in it, want only a taste, probably, before

they turn back to whatever shore they keep.

THE GREAT BIG JAGGED PIECE OF PAIN

Cynthia Cahn

jerked from its fitting
place in you
grows panicky black

wings the better
to knock around your
bone cage with

blind stupid needle
beak foraging
you can be doing the

calmest things
type a memo
plan strategies at

the pool table
tour a museum
bend down to look

in your oven and all
this time this clawing
screeching hell

EBB TIDE (Route 92)

Cynthia Cahn

The road spills into you
as if world peeled
its skin back, yielding
a lush green heart;

mangroves prevail,
frothed up from baywater;
leaves, branches tangle,
chaos of bristling lace —

and under water's glaze
flat muck packed with
fists of old roots
pushing.

NOBODY COMPARES
WAVES TO BAYONETS

Cynthia Cahn

Since then it's been harder
to tuck the screams in, button
my scars, hang all that
ecstacy out to dry till
next time.

The real world wants my skin
bumless, my voice
white sugar. I want to
redefine "real."

Through me. Again. Yes,
through, right up to the light
behind light. I learn
the meaning of lasers,

even when dance
floors fold like sheets, leaving
ache, my cells, dreams
hoard it: This is

how sun must feel,
I say:
crazily wheeling its blue groove
down, heeling at nothing, hawks
in tow, swans,
dragonflies, all things flying.

Cynthia Cahn

On TV the squat gray basket-weaver
county matriarch, grandchild of slaves
chops saplings, hauls them home, strips them.

In the valley outside, its trash
and tangles of frost-browned tough
kudzu, thrash two cats mating.

Plump wrinkled fingers, calloused, graced
with generations of craft, plait
band after pliant bright band into shape.

That pair means business:
he bites down, rasps in her belly;
her claws dig, scrabble in dead leaves, grit.

This artisan is the last, and knows it.
Her deep voice quivers a hymn like frail
wind-struck wire shimmering in sun.

and from fanged maws' rough-tongued dark
rise long squalls lashing with aimless barbs
ripping the paint off night.

FORTY FOUR QUARTERS

Donald Caswell

The coke machine broke with a rattling crunch
like the sound of a freight train buckling up
and coins burst from the coin return slot
covering the concrete floor. We scooped
handfuls and divided: David got the dimes
because there were so many, Alan
got the nickels because
we were bigger than he was, and I
instinctively opted for the quarters
though they seemed so rare. David made
eight bucks, Alan less than five. And I
walked off with forty four quarters
and a chance to finally
be somebody.
          No, Officer, I do not
honestly believe that the magnet
tied to the end of a string
which we dropped like a hand line
into the hole below the bottle opener
to fish for bottle caps
could have seriously affected
the coin return mechanism. Bottle caps,
Sir. If you find one with a red star
they give you a new bicycle.

Imagine how things might have been
beginning life with forty four quarters
in a leather bag, slung round my neck
like a good luck charm. I could have been
in great demand at all night laundromats
and toll booths. Winos, knowing intuitively
of my good luck, would have tapped my cache
for phone calls, cups of coffee, alleged
bus rides home, the odd honest drunk
straight out begging for a bottle of Black Jack.

My friends would have bummed quarters for beers,
pool games, cigarette machines, my quarters
dwindling rapidly while I waited for the day
I'd meet the woman of my dreams
and need all forty four quarters
and my pocket change to feed
condom vending machines.

 All this I lost
when the coke machine broke and filled my world
with the glittering promise of acquired wealth
the tease of get-rich-quick.

         Cops pulled up outside.
We knew they'd make us give the money back
and maybe take our bottle caps away.
David ran. Alan turned white and tears
began to form at the edges of his eyes.
I assayed the situation — the flashing light
out front, the lack of adequate emergency
egress — reached deep into my pocket
for a single coin
placed it in the appropriate slot
and bought a coke.

Donald Caswell

I cannot tell you what it means to be
a member of my generation
except to say that a young boy
could sleep on a bicycle
riding home from a public pool,
exhausted by hours in the water,
luminous with lassitude,
yet able to pedal and steer in his sleep
through the wide streets
of Coral Gables, clouds building
out to sea, the breeze threatening
thunder and rain, smells of crotons,
hibiscus, jasmine stirring his lizard brain
while the unwritten history of chaos
lingered in the distance, waiting
to swallow the dreams of a generation
with no memory of killing, wanting only
to take another leap from the high platform,
one more lap around the swimming pool.

Donald Caswell

— *after Nicanor Parra*

Our teachers drove us nuts
with their irrelevant questions:
Who is the author
of *The Four Horsemen of the Apocalypse?*
What are three factors of thirty times three?
Where did Cervantes write *Don Quixote?*
When will we see another eclipse?
Why doesn't the Tower of Pisa fall over?
And how do you explain
the hydrostatic paradox?

The real truth of the matter
is that we couldn't have cared less.
We were men of action.
All their lectures and all their tests
were only pauses between the games.
Kickball, dodgeball, football, baseball.
We knew the world was round. That's why
we left it in our glove at night — to
give the pocket shape. We knew friction
and gravity were the two things
man had to overcome in order to fly
into space. That's why
we gave each other Indian burns
and spit off balconies.

Yet they kept hammering at us anyway:
the skeletal structure of the komodo dragon
the electromagnetic theory of light
the component parts of the dicotyledons
the etymology of the word *Gesundheit*

And least favorite of all, from first
grade up, the question I hated worst:
What will you be when you grow up?
When you grow up, what will you be?

I'd rather have had the earth
swallow me up than answer that
question. I'd rather have been impaled
on a burning stake. What are my choices?
To be a bootlicking toady to whatever
pea-brained miscreant inherits the business?
To rebel against oppression and guarantee
myself a lifetime without freedom
or happiness? To say what I think
and lose all my friends?
To drink until my liver explodes?

Oh, I know what they wanted to hear.
But can you imagine a healthy child
actually giving a damn what's in store
for him in three decades?
Not when there are waves to splash in.
Not when a turtle lugs its heavy shell
out of the drainage ditch and races
across the street in slow motion.
Ooh, that car came close.

When I grow up I will be ... a ... a
grown-up. In the meantime
I'm going to take the top off this anthill
just to make sure
there are ants inside.

But the questions kept coming:
Who discovered the Lesser Antilles?

What is the major cause of gout?
Where is the rest of the unfinished symphony?
How did Hannibal cross the Alps?
Why are you moaning and putting your head down?
And what will you be, will you be, will you be?
What will you be, will you be?

I probably shouldn't blame the teachers.
To them, the world was a series of ladders
on which we climb till we reach the top
or until our heart and lungs give out
whichever comes first. To them, these questions
were the difference between poverty
and the material heaven of the bourgeoisie.
Still, they might have taken the time
to try to see the world from my side of
the fence. In my little world,
no one was dead yet, except the ones
who had always been dead. In my world,
the social order was clearly defined:
stay away from the big guys and never
hit a girl. Trees were a means
of transportation, and the need to defecate
was no reason to be alone.
Come on in and keep me company.

What was the need for all their questions?
Couldn't they just tell us straight out
instead of expecting us to think up
everything ourselves?
The New World was discovered in 1492.
(The Old World has yet to be discovered.)
Population is expanding at a geometric rate,
food production linearly. Darwin
was right — we're apes with good breeding.

The sun is a ball of fire so hot
its heat travels 93 million miles
and is still strong enough
to make the sweat run into your eyes
each time you bend over to tie
your shoes. You're gonna need to do
that left one again. It's still loose.

Now hurry up inside and clean the erasers.
Get your books out and start reading.
I don't want to hear any talking.
A math test does not require conversation.

Did they think we were passing nuclear
secrets? A math test
isn't exactly a funeral. Unless
we're talking about the death of innocence
and love for life lived for itself.
And when you grow up you will be
a narrow-minded pedagogue, just like me.

But no, they just kept hammering at us:
Where is the line between work and distraction?
How will I know when I'm acting like me?
When will time be the only dimension?
What is the French for ennui?
And why is there only one word for thesaurus?

In the meantime, Viet Nam.
In the meantime, the national debt.
Adolescence — fear, lust, and confusion.
Youth — under the table, drunk.
Maturity — never to be, never to be.
And old age — always waiting,
downstage in the darkness with insect wings.

Donald Caswell

To be always seeking after the useful
does not become free and exalted souls.
— Aristotle

The poet who roughs his hands on wood
Making dovetails, dados, miters, and butts,
Will never awe critics with his clever use
Of the anapest, nor one day find

A poem he'd forgotten writing
Clinging to the back pages
Of some dusty journal, an obscure
Footnote in free verse, and a welcome

Addition to his curriculum vita.
At noon the poet who works in wood
Scribbles on a paper bag,
Iambic lines that will never see

The inside of a book, or be seen
By anyone who writes reviews,
Rhymes that never work
They way he wants them to,

No matter how many times
He scratches out a line and tries again.
Sawdust clings to the backs of hands
That can separate ash from oak by feel

And build a box that locks without a key,
A puzzle in three dimensions, six sides
Sanded so smooth no one can find
The seams that tie them all together.

IN THE STYLE OF TU FU
AT CHRISTMAS TIME IN KANSAS CITY

Donald Caswell

Gazing at the Lights on the Plaza
What is the god of commerce like?
An unending display of colored lights.
Swelling crowds sweep by. Returning
Shoppers block streets and walks.
One day soon, from the top
of the Ritz, these countless points
of useless beauty will be small enough
to hold in a single glance.

Restless Night
Smells of sulphur and coffee
Drift through the garden.
Moonlight floods the patio:
Snow-covered woodpile,
An ancient iron gear beneath
A frozen waterfall, not turning,
Far from any factory, with no
Apparent purpose.

Full Moon after First Snow
Road still dark, but everything else white,
A twice-sized moon casts moist shadows
On empty buildings. Above night-filled
Offices, a single bull stands sentinel
On his tower, facing into the wind.
Beneath his vacant gaze, the moon's
Reflection in the river goes unnoticed,
Defeated by glittering casino lights.

Day's End
Phones stopped ringing long ago.
The computer monitor is dark.
Sirens call me from the street.
Winter rain fills the gutters.
My hair seems whiter tonight
In the glow from the fireplace.
Logs hiss and spit, flames
Flickering a semaphore — Good
Fortune — over and over.
For whom and for what?

THE PROPER MOTION OF THE SUN

Donald Caswell

The circumference of a circle holds
its beginning and its end.
　　　— Heraclitus

The proper motion of the sun cannot be
Inferred from a single glance. Nor can
The fundamental truth of the earth, wet
Beneath us, cold and hot and cold again,
The beginning and the end of all we know.

What does philosophy matter to the hand
With the trowel, pulling up dark soil, dropping
A seed, and closing up the hole? Water
Is needed, and the earth must spin two dozen
Times before a shoot will show. But for now

We're only planting seeds in the midday,
Midsummer, southern Florida sun: five
White boys, eight blacks, and a one-handed
Seminole. What forces make us what we are?

As with a single mind, fourteen near-strangers
Bend in the searing heat, eyes filled with sweat,
Feeling our way along the ground, row by row,
Until the sun sinks into the trees and the boss calls us
To the water truck, to pay us off and send us home.

TWO OUT, TWO ON,
TYING RUN AT THE PLATE

Donald Caswell

High, Inside Fastball

Has the awkward rhythm of a foreign tongue.
It's technically correct, but takes too long
To say. If that's what's on your mind
You'll never get out of the box in time.
You need the instant measure of vernacular:
Beanball, chin music, wake-up call.
Leave the play-by-play to the man in the booth.
Hit the dirt. Hug your shoes.

Roundhouse Curve, Low and Away

The curveball drops more than it curves,
But its curve is more than illusion,
Unlike the rising fastball, which merely sinks
More slowly than most fast pitches. It's academic.
Your turning shoulder has written a fate
That all your piety and wit cannot erase
As the ball sails three inches beyond
And five below your useless bat. Strike one.

Fastball at the hands.

Because you can't extend your arms
For a full-strength swing, they say
The pitcher jams your hands. You can
Try to foul this one off, but it's definitely
In your kitchen. Just hope you don't break
Your bat and that it doesn't actually jam
Your hand against the bat, hitting your
Knuckles instead of the wood. Don't take
This one for the team. Let it go. Strike two.

Slider in the dirt.
On the bases, all sliders are in the dirt.
At the plate, a fast curve can be
Anywhere. This one is digging a hole,
Bringing the catcher to his knees
To block the ball with his chest
While you hold one hand up to stop
The runners, who aren't running
Anyway, lest eagerness and bad base
Running let a close game slip away.

Painting the outside corner.
On every pitch, the story is the same:
He wants you to swing at nothing, or wait
While a big, bright melon crawls across the plate.
You know his aim and everything he throws —
Fastball, curveball, slider, change — though
Whatever comes will come as a surprise,
If not for you, for the other guy. To swing
Or not to swing. You have seven hundredths
Of a second to make up your mind. Too late.
Game over. Struck out looking. Ʞ.

FOR MARY LYNNE
(AT 4 IN THE MORNING)

Valerie Chronis Bickett

Think of the fat pines 20 miles west
of the sand roads white in the moon
Chuck-will's-widows in the Scrub Oaks

Think of the interstate, of the tunnel in Mobile
of my grandmother in Birmingham asleep on the double bed
in the back room, of the Vulcan with his traffic light
Think of the curve the Mississippi makes
under New Orleans, the ugliness of a city
where nothing is underground
The Atchafalaya, the road on the levy into Rose
Think of the Rothko chapel in Houston
in the subdivisions near the hospitals
of my father waiting for his operation
in the morning

Think of Cincinnati, the bright White Castle on Vine
the clean warm hold the men there
have on their cups of coffee
the view from my bathroom
of Kentucky

Think of Kansas, Nebraska
of still Iowa towns. Houses across the street
from fields of corn, porch lights
that have been turned off

Think of Larry and his girlfriend living south
of Calgary, of Banff, of Sausalito
where I was conceived, of Madeline in Hawaii
and the birth control pills she still
has her mother send her from Cleveland

Think of Greece, of the road down from Athens
through Nauplion and Leonidion to Apithia
of the sun just now pink on the cantaloupes

It is not just one man
and one woman
who marry
You are lover
to many men
each one with the name of Rodney
When one of them says
I need to see another woman
and they take a vote on it
and leave
and the house is quiet
recognize now the shy women
with their hands raised
in the back of the room
each one with the name of Mary Lynne

Valerie Chronis Bickett

The banks of my heart drip red mud
The nickelodeon plays Scheherazade
The cherubim   the seraphim   the whores
They make the river rise

Your heart nourishes floods
The humming   the pre-menstrual
ringing of the tidal wave in the pulse
Honey or self-portraits or someone else
sandbag the bruises

My blood lies in you flood plain
You rise and the color changes
You rise higher
The trees are red
You crest
It's a tight fit

Your flow is as innocent
as my boundaries
Your backwaters come to me
as relief
You drain
what I can't hold any longer

To the rain
to the springs
to the creeks that feed you
to the oceans that finally dilute you
you laugh with your mouth open
Me
you watch
waiting for a dam

River River River
your waves all in my lap
a thousand of your tongues in my ear
I am inundated inundated with you
You are red red with mud
The cherubim the seraphim the whores
They make the river rise
They make the river fall

THE OTHER SNAKE

Valerie Chronis Bickett

She is under one rock

                                       I am under another

She is only a Queen

                 My hourglass figure ends in a copper head

She calls me to her hole

She wants to kiss me through the curtain

                              I think of my venom

She says you have let her go

                               It has been a while now

                since you took me home in a pillow sack

You have let her go she says

                                    I shiver

You don't want to see her anymore

Everyone throws her back

She says that you have let her go

That your hands felt warm

She asks if my scales rot too

                      I illustrate my speech defect

                            with goose bumps

                  I tell her to go play volleyball

                 I direct her to Reelfoot Lake

                 I hum Yankee Doodle Dandy

She cries

                        I inquire about her sinuses

She laughs

                             I catch myself

She sheds her skin

                               I call you

Valerie Chronis Bickett

Let's talk about what happens
when you kiss me that way —
full, with intent, softness,
lightness. Taking time.
There with two minutes
before we have to leave to do
something I have proposed
which you said you were willing to do,
join forces with me early in the morning
in a task, because we were after all
riding high on several days of closeness,
nothing between us there that morning.

Let's talk now
about what I did, how I felt
there in bed so caught
on the hook of some forgotten
breaking point; otherwise, why
when I started to kiss back, return it
in kind, give you back what you ask for,
let you in other words run your tongue
over my lips and through them, glaze
my mouth, receive your stepping out
to meet me with the necessary reply.
I can't do it.

I can't do it but I do
for a few minutes, pretend,
drop anchor, jump ship,
swim around in cold water
for awhile and watch the two of us
with no words for what I see
until I can't stand it anymore and say,
"We need to get going."

and take my mouth off yours
the way I pick up the telephone.

It shouldn't have surprised me then
that the next time you and I meet alone,
everyone gone or asleep,
there in the living room at eleven
that night you turn your back to me
until I say something and take you
into court at the kitchen table
to try to work it out.
Stupid we both say
there with fifteen ghosts of the past
jangling their chains for every hopeful
spirit of the future —
not five feet away from cuts in the linoleum
you made when you threw that mug
one night to make your point,
in sight of the famous bathroom standoff
when I wouldn't let you brush your teeth
in peace, but betting against the odds
we slog it out, my style so ostensibly ministerial,
so full of the Girl Scout pledge.
and you the silent bully, limp, making
such a show of indifference, eyelids up and down.

How to account for the lack of bloodshed then,
our bodies perched on fear trying once again
to start at the beginning, unravel,
why you, why I, felt angry.
I tell you I wanted so badly for you to work with me;
you tell me I wanted so badly for you to bite
a rotten apple and I tell you it was golden
and you say it was rotten
and I ask you why you just didn't say something and

you say you did and we yawn and I take
the softer of the two pomegranates
on the table in front of us and a knife
and eat some of the sharp fruit I like so much
and I know you don't and say goodnight

and I am up early thinking of how much work
it is to stay in this and I go back
to the kiss, that rotten apple
you wanted me to bite yesterday morning
and I think of the shivers
it gave me, such a mix of pleasure
and pain, the presence of this state
of affairs in a long marriage
no one told me about, and I think
of your need to make nonsense of everything
and at the first hint of trouble
to return to the womb and
of my need to make sense of everything,
not just kiss each hurt,
but slide my tongue in between
each fiery wound.

THE GOODBYE THAT GOT STUCK IN MY THROAT

Valerie Chronis Bickett

for my mother

As you fly away
I am cooking greens
in my kitchen —
sun pouring in,
blue jays and preschoolers squawking
across the street.
You sit buckled in,
ready for take-off,
the fan supplying you the air
you are trying hard to remember
to breathe in from your belly.
Weeks of anxiety
coming to this.

How is it that we got so hurt,
you and I,
that we can't take in
the ordinary disappointments,
see in the dark?
We lust for comfort; it seems
we can't survive discomfort.
Life or death. Everything,
life or death.

This time of year your mother
would go crazy for greens, *vleeta,*
go out digging in the empty lots,
places she'd spot by the side of the road.
Come back with grocery bags full
and start sifting through the leaves,
cutting off the roots
washing off the dirt.

We peasant people weren't meant for flying,
not meant for empty condos in Cambridge either,
the ethereal land around Harvard.
Come back home.
Let's live like the sisters we are,
tease each other about our personal dramas
while we move in and out of the seasons
we both have left together.

In the kitchen garden
I imagine us working on together
we can be side by side
like the song said,
coax color out of the ground
and sit back and look at what comes,
this garden a third woman
who keeps trying to catch our eye.

ESCAPING THE SEA

Mary Ann Coleman

Tidewaters of the Atlantic
skim twilight to shore.
Waves lapse to the sea's hollow.
Snail shells, oysters, jingles
flow toward us, spin and are gone.
Sandpiper's prints, tracks of fiddler crab.

Clouds shift on the intricate sand.

Floating in your arms
that rock like rented boats
I want to live forever, think
of the dorsal fins of shark
lifting out of rough water.

Come, I'll give you
a conch shell for our aging house,
a ghost sound of the sea.

Mary Ann Coleman

I row in high wind,
coax the boat beyond pines
that creak like rocking chairs.

Islands grow in my eyes;
pig plant, moss, wild iris.
Tap roots feel under the loose loam
for hidden messages.

Once I rowed
past the calls of parents
to swim where weeds
curved out of dark waters
vining around my legs
to pull me down.

Wanting to go back
I lean toward those
old river weeds.
Land begins to inch
past my shoulders.
My paddle falls, floats
where night grows under maples.
The boat drifts to the center of the lake,
the water under the bow
talking, talking,
crowded with its own mouths.

STILL LIFE WITH RAIN AND NECTARINES

Mary Ann Coleman

On a winter day
a bowl of nectarines rests on a kitchen table,
alizarin crimson swirling through egg-yellow.
Colors that, opposing, intensify
and warm the mind of the woman who sits, alone,
in her customary place, centering on the fruit.

There is, of course, the rain
she quarrels with.

Just past the sliding glass door,
a continual fall from a sky
gone pewter gray
and small holding pools
on the porch
where a mason
failed to utilize his level.

Thin lines of rain
stream from neglected gutters
as she sees a time
when the cement will craze,
slough off in pieces like a jigsaw puzzle,
jackhammers pound the porch to stony rubble
and other women sit inside this room.

Still, she lingers near the fruit as she recalls
the day she and her son stood on the porch
and she asked him, "What do you believe?"
"In this," he said, "All this!"
gesturing to the pines swaying in the wind,
the sun, the summer sky.

Though her house should fall completely,
she thinks such moments
must surely charge the landscape
in the same way a rainbow has
of forming colors the human eye
can't see but senses
all the same — a gentle pressure
with just the force
of a bowl of nectarines
raging on a kitchen table
under a roof hammered by winter rain.

Mary Ann Coleman

— for Guy Owen

January
Dead. You are dead.
I burn my returned letter.
Flames chatter and leap
as my words char
in the precise flame.
The delicate tissue twists,
lifts in a slight breeze.
Gases and ash
drift over these ochre hills.

February
As I sit by a leaf-stained pool,
a film on the water
like the dull underside of foil
breaks. Scale-flash of gold.
A fish arcs and vanishes
as lily pads pulse.
I think of the way you stirred,
gesturing in the lecture hall.

A breeze shifts the pines
as though from the hand of a god
involved with other matters.
The cold world shudders slowly
toward some improbable spring.
A spring remote as the night
we listened to folk songs
sitting on a creaking, wooden floor.
Why did you hide the news
of your coming death?
Words familiar to you
as the articulate tongue
in your warm and dying mouth.

September
Months I would not, could not
think of you, summer
staggering these houses
with its tons of flowers.
Teacher, writer, friend —
I still hear you say
"catch the bear in the forest of words."

Then death burned your cancerous flesh clean.

Through the sloughing off of months,
I watch a gradual edge of change
travel the incendiary leaves
as I write,
still prowling the dense,
heart-shaking forest
you knew so well.

The cobalt sky intensifies.
The autumn sun
splinters through the polished
needles of pines.
Riding on that fire,
you slide past,
slip inside my shoulders,
my pale skin.

I am your body now.

Burning with that knowledge,
I close my pen.
Then, remembering the fugitive bear,
I open it again.

ON WATCHING
"THE MARTIAN CHRONICLES"

Mary Ann Coleman

as he looked through the telescope
from Mars, he saw the earth explode

In Bradbury's work
we find the way horror grows —
not through fantasy alone
but in the imagination
linked to the entirely possible.
An understanding: flame issuing from our children's eyes,
their flesh cracking, sliding off like lizard skin.
Grandchildren locked in charred wombs
for all unrecorded time.
Trees, blackened veins on a burning sky
Cumulus clouds of fire.
Where the serene lake rocked, a crater of coals,
the million spontaneous deaths of wild flowers.

Never again the sudden scatter of rain
in a hot, dry season,
the ocean's push and withdrawing moan,
the early morning sun on the sides
of old brick buildings,
goldfish rising in ponds
like cool trombone notes.

After the consuming wind,
mountains of ash.
The earth
a bloodstone,
a dim, unimaginable star.

THE DAY MOTHER BUTTERED HER PURSE

Mary Ann Coleman

— for Austen

Oh, there was a morning stranger than all
the mornings I've ever known.
Breakfast time looked like midnight,
we couldn't see the sun.

My brother shrank into the toaster
and everything got worse,
our frog dressed up in a silly hat
and Mother buttered her purse.

At that, Dad's eggs marched across the stove,
his coffee changed to mud
and snowflakes floated from our mouths
with everything we said.

Our house turned into a dinosaur
and as we rode on his scaly back
our driveway squeezed into a toothpaste tube
and the sky began to crack.

But I jumped to the ground and began to draw
on the sky with my ball point pen
and the day grew back with the sun I'd made
and time was right again.

So I guard the egg carton with both eyes
remembering that awful curse
when the sky grew black in the morning
and Mother buttered her purse.

BAMBOO WOMEN

Gary Corseri

I dream of bamboo women:
slender, arching reeds along the river bank,
swaying long lean bodies
as yellow as the face of China.

During the monsoon,
bending at the waist,
they seem to break,
only to surprise the laughing sun.

They have survived ten thousand storms
in just this fashion.
They will survive ten thousand more.
A playful child,

fearful of tigers,
hides among their green and yellow dresses.
The warm waters cover him.
He drinks air through a woman's body.

BLUE PARROT

Gary Corseri

I love you ...
because you are tall.
because your dark hair
rests on your shoulders
as simply as blackbirds
that sing on a mountain.

because you drink
café au lait
slow as an emerald lizard,
and, if you spoke,
you would speak only French
and I would never understand you.

mostly, though,
because you sit in a corner
in a dark room
behind dark glasses;
and, if the rain fell suddenly,
because you would smile.

Gary Corseri

So who else should it be at that hour of the night,
out in the country like I am, except …
Geronimo — standing there with his headband in his hand,
still bloody from the latest buffalo kill,
asking me sheepishly if he can use the phone.

So I say, "Why sure, Geronimo!" and he cha-chas
across the living room, *huya-huyaing*,
and I pour him some firewater
and the two of us get sentimental and start to sing
Deutschland, Deutschland über alles.

Later on, we have a heart to heart no forked-tongue
blood-brother talk about the Old West.
And the old bear shakes his head,
he gets this faraway look in his eyes,
he *huya-huyas* a few more times,
and then he melts into the living room carpet,
and he doesn't even leave a stain.

Gary Corseri

Once in Japan I saw
two old ladies polishing wood.
The centuries had made it smooth
as the bronze temple bells;

even the gold Buddha stood
immaculate in the morning air
as the sun scaled the tall bamboo
and fell in a waterfall.

Upon their knees they worked
with bandanas around their hair,
barely pausing to look
how the deep green paled in the moss,

or what exotic head
the feet on the stairs might carry.
They were like lanterns of stone
who moved as the light might move them —

so still — yet, so steady the sweep
of cloth on the polished wood,
the sun went blue as I watched them,
the bamboo wept like the blind.

Gary Corseri

They bring home the body of *Jesús el canario*.
Nine years old, with a bullet in his throat.
See where the bullet caught *Jesús* in midflight.
And the song seeped out like a bloody flag.

His father is holding *Jesús el canario*.
For a thousand years he must carry this corpse.
A woman stands in the doorway, weeping:
one hand over her breast,

one over her mouth,
singing the one ineluctable song
while the soft feathers brush the skin of *Jesús*
and the doorways shudder in the living hearts.

She should not weep for him, this woman,
foolish as all women, with the womb's grieving
foolishness for life — O soft nurture
of the womb's feathers brushing the dreaming skin!

In the barrios they wait for *los pumas* —
assassins, dark angels, avengers of dreams.
They hate *Jesús* and all singing.
They shoot the sperm of death, and sleep calmly.

In the courtyard runs the fragrance of the roses:
wine-dark and apolitical,
in a vase of sun-palmed water —
water warm as blood.

AN AMARANTH FOR CHICO

Gary Corseri

They burn down the Amazon, Chico!
Serengueiros run for cover, cattle ranchers
pave roads over rubber trees, burn up ozone,
sour the wild winds.
Pistoleros stalk you where you sleep,
pistoleros mortgage dreams, grin bullets,
abort air with the stink of rubber
rising over el Planalto de Matto Grosso.

From Acre to Belo Horizonte, across Rondonia:
sabers of roads where tributaries spilled
molten silver under cobalt skies,
where red dolphins cavorted
ten thousand times ten thousand years:
tractors claw the livelihood, white sap seeps
like tears of Christ of the outstretched arms —
too far to catch your riddled body
fallen in the house of your children,
too far to catch in vessels of gold
your bloodlike rubies.

They are killing us all, Chico Mendez!
Insatiably ripping the silk from the sky
while dust rises in nostrils of children,
covers the amethyst sea,
settles on white lips of the Sudan,
fills the distended bodies of the Sahara,
while fly-sodden *olvidados* sweep
desert roads for seed.
In the leaves of the rubber trees,
in Amazon tributaries
your clear silver voice cascades,
breaks over moribund cities
washes the *favelas* clean.

Churning the Gulf Stream,
roiling the Rio Grande,
surging the Mississippi —
jeweled-blue-planet-crying-in-the-wilderness song.

They burn down the Amazon, Chico!
Stars glitter like tambourines
held by gypsies singing by nightfires
lighting cities' hills.
Fireflies gather at the ears of children,
into dark chambers of inner ears
whisper your phosporescent name
incessantly ...
incessantly ...
incessantly ...

Gary Corseri

Her mind is no less than the autumn light
upon the heirlooms that arrange her home
upon the hill that overlooks the sea.
Like polished silver in the peace of night
that warms us with the full moon's calm,
she has enriched her memory
by constant questioning — and being free.
Only such a one is bound to keep
the soared songs of our common lot assayed,
and chart us to our end by being brave.
She is the balancer who cannot reap
the harvest of our best, unless it's played
upon the anthems of our dawn — nor save
a stitch in time, unless we move towards love.

Gary Corseri

It is the attack of the ripened moment:
latticed bones of the poised hand
strung to the brush above paper;
the brush recalls swatting flies
above the rump, the ox's bellow
on rocks below, silver falls above.

Day after day the artist seems
mesmerized by blankness:
a wanderer staring at snow.

When he is easy in this wandering,
when the sense of the lost self is lost
and all is recalled in a moment —
the paper leaps
to catch the latticed bones,
the oxtail's flicker licks
illuminating silence.

Call it "Spirit Resonance" —
the *ch'i* of the Breath of Heaven
blown across a bamboo copse,
rippling a blank, white sea.

ON A PRINT BY HIROSHIGE

Gary Corseri

for Yoko

The print by Hiroshige
hangs on the wall
in the bedroom where you're absent.

I remember the day your father
withdrew from his reliquary
these peasants in the snow.
Though it was his favorite
he gave it smiling,
and under it you and I
made love the night we parted.

Three weather-beaten peasants
part from one another
as the village darkens and brightens
in the hallowed light of the snow.
Wherever they wander —
however far from earshot —
snow shoulders their footsteps,
spreads like the bridal gown
of the Empress of Night.

Nothing's older than loneliness,
nothing more durable.
The old artist knew it
as a purity
we dare not lie down within:
a swirling —
cooling and burning at once.

We are passing, regardless,
with the live bones inside us
dreaming of snow.

WHAT MUSIC IS

Silvia Curbelo

*While dissident poet Angel Cuadra was serving time in Cuba's Boniato
prison, his poems were smuggled out of the country inside a guitar.*

Nest in the rafters, birdsong,
what the neighbor girl heard
one morning from her narrow bed
dreaming by the book, his own
eyes lifted to the racket of sparrows
in the yard, a sack of marbles
in his pocket, a whole bright
constellation of them, first the blue ones,
then the red. Sun landing on his brother's
boat shoes, the hand-me-down
clothes he wore, looking for his father's
keys, his mother's empty veils, a closet full
of dresses, rose shadowed, humming.

Days spent in the quiet schoolhouse,
landlocked, swimming by booklight, so many
bright fish in the sea, the salty
cupboards smeared with flour, leaving
white footprints on his grandmother's porch,
up till all hours, moonlight hissing
in the yard and a train in the distance.
Writing in window dust, *Te espero, escucha,*
books heavy on his back all the way

down the beach, the satchel light
he carried, the sea at night, every wave
a long road to a morning of boats circling
in the sun, empty, cut loose,

the mother's hum, the widow's wail,
while music wafts all night through the sleeping
house. Branches swaying to the tapping
of rain on a tin roof, heavy as moonlight
rattling the loose boards, cracking
the windows open, what he knew was coming,

the overturned furniture of years,
clocks with their hands ripped out,
still ticking, still alive,

then gone. Doing time in the swampland, road
following the river, becoming the river, turning
brackish along the white stones.
Trail song, wish song,
the bed of light he climbed out of
early one morning in the room where she slept,
the chair where he left her and
the chair where he found her
years later clutching some makeshift
flag, his own torn sleeve.

Then counting the white caps off
Boniato island, each wave
a hand, each hand
a fist, what music is finally
among the gray stones, scrape
of stubble in the prison yard
and a love like felled trees, ghost
kiss from nowhere.

Silvia Curbelo

In every half-filled glass a river
begging to be named, rain on a leaf,
a snowdrift. What we long for

precedes us. What we've lost
trails behind, casting
a long shadow. Tonight

the music's sad, one man's
outrageous loneliness detonated
into arpeggios of relief. The way

someone once cupped someone's
face in their hands, and the world
that comes after. Everything

can be pared down to gravity
or need. If the soul soars with longing
the heart plunges headfirst

into what's left, believing
there's a pure want
to fall through. What we drink to

in the end is loss, the space
around it, the opposite
of thirst, its shadow.

TONIGHT I CAN ALMOST HEAR THE SINGING

Silvia Curbelo

There is a music to this sadness.
In a room somewhere two people dance.
I do not mean to say desire is everything.
A cup half empty is simply half a cup.
How many times have we been there and not there?
I have seen waitresses slip a night's
worth of tips into the jukebox, their eyes
saying *yes* to nothing in particular.
Desire is not the point.
Tonight your name is a small thing
falling through sadness. We wake alone
in houses of sticks, of straw, of wind.
How long have we stood at the end of the pier
watching that water going?
In the distance the lights curve along
Tampa Bay, a wishbone ready to snap
and the night riding on that half promise,
a half moon to light the whole damned sky.
This is the way things are with us.
Sometimes we love almost enough.
We say *I can do this, I can do*
more than this and faith feeds
on its own version of the facts.
In the end the heart turns on itself
like hunger to a spoon.
We make a wish in a vanishing landscape.
Sadness is one more reference point
like music in the distance.
Two people rise from a kitchen table
as if to dance. What do they know
about love?

TOURISM IN THE LATE 20TH CENTURY

Silvia Curbelo

Blue boat of morning and already
the window is besieged
by sky. Grace takes no prisoners
in a town like this. Think of the girl
sipping white burgundy
in the local café, her straw hat
with its pale flower, indigenous
and small as the white roll
she's buttering one philosophical
corner at a time. Even the rain
that falls some afternoons here
is more conceptual, more a tribute
to rain than actual rain falling
on the tulips, a rumor
the wind carries all the way
down the beach.
And would you ask the sea
to explain itself? wrote Kerouac once
in a book about a woman
who was already a metaphor,
rose fading in its glass bowl.
He always knew the world is sentimental,
waving its lacy rags over the face
of the familiar, an architecture
of piano notes and hope.
Imagine the girl, her hat gone,
her bread finished, holding out
an armful of tulips in the rain.
She knows each road leads
to other roads, to small towns
with solid names like *Crestview* and
Niceville where even dust has
a genealogy and an address,
as if there's more forever there.

The tulips long to be metaphysical,
closed-mouthed, more faithful
than the rose. Let the windows
take over. Lean out the small
square of the day, past
the rain, past the idea
of rain, to where the sky
is snapshot blue, the sea
blue by association.

LEARNING TO PLAY COLTRANE

Silvia Curbelo

She thought it was green, not
the emerald green of Indian summer
but a green like a darkening plain,
or the shadow rivers cast.
She thought it was light, a glint
of a warning, the shine
at the papery edge
of storm clouds. The way
a voice rising and falling becomes
a premonition, a dampness
at the back of her neck. Or maybe
it was more of an imprint,
a memory of sound, some afternoon
after the circus has left town
and all that remains is a field
strewn with garbage, a music
of pasted stars and ruin.
And she thought of a color
like that, mud-green, the green
of a small sadness, shapeless
as the wind itself. And for a moment
she owned everything inside it,
the light, the field, the wind.
                    — *for Adrian*

Silvia Curbelo

It's not the way the light haunts
that particular landscape, or how clouds

in the distance imitate the world at rest.
The way the curtains hold the late

afternoon is not an issue. It's not
the lilies abandoned on the table,

or the dog lying beside her, or the wine.
It's not the weight of memory

on his eyelids. It's not the empty cup
he carries walking home in the dark

through fields brimming with sleep,
or the precarious raft of her

mouth on his, or her hands
in the evenings

putting cold cream where her youth had been.

THIS POEM IS MISSING

Silvia Curbelo

The difference between a mountain
and an abyss is a question of perspective.

Every mirror is an island
we're rowing toward.

Look how this moment disappears behind a cloud.
I never said the world was substantial.

Even as it conceals it,
the glove imitates the hand.

The air around a flower
is also the flower.

A basket of roses speaks for itself.
Silence is another thing altogether.

If nothing falls in the forest
does it matter who isn't there to listen?

Sorrows outnumber trees.
A man drinks to his orphaned heart

and swallows the voice
of what is missing.

The poem inside the mirror is
no dream, but tell me,

who will console the dreamer?

IN THE LAND OF MISSED CHANCES

Silvia Curbelo

There was no news
in God's country. The sun
sank without warning.
Every ship sailed away.

No one sang for her supper
or looked for answers in the stars
or prayed for rain.
No one poured the last wine.
The dispossessed left nothing
in their wake.

There were no telephones
ringing, no music playing.
Nothing bloomed in the yard.
No one was lost or blamed
or left for dead.

There were no crimes to speak of.
The cops found no fresh signs
of struggle, no blood on
the sheets, no lipstick-stained
cigarettes still smoldering in
ashtrays. No one gave up
the ghost or fell from grace.

Nobody rolled the dice
or held the winning card.
The last of our luck ran out,
swallowed the key
and closed the book.
We didn't have a prayer.

THE GILL NETTERS

Robert Dana

An odd one. A kind of sea-
going John-boat. Twenty
feet long and Navy grey.
Maybe an eight- or nine-foot
beam. Very shallow draft
to work that close to shore.
And no cockpit. Instead,
a kind of narrow conning
tower open to the weather.
Up there, her skipper sits
hatless, in an orange slicker
working throttle and wheel
and wireless phone. No
name lettered astern. No
My Money or Sea Queen or Wet
Dreams. No port of origin.
Just a row of plain black
numbers stencilled on her bow.

The morning's cold rains had
tailed off, leaving the Gulf
sky, the sand, the water all
a marly agate. Then we saw
her anchor-buoy a yard off
shore like a lost basketball;
the boat awash in a trough
behind the sandbar; lengths
of net paying out across her
transom through the hands
of two men in yellow slicker
pants held up by braces. One,
moustached; one under a red,
billed cap. Both strong
armed and sun-dark. Cubans,
maybe. Francisco. Manuel.

Patiently setting a double,
coil, a weir, a labyrinth of
perhaps a hundred yards of
clear monofilament, its rosary
of cork floats riding the swells.

There's wind, of course, light
now, and South-southwest — up
from Havana and the Keys — and
a few last spits of rain.
"Time spent fishing cannot
be deducted from a man's soul,"
someone said. Tell that to the
dolphins cruising the sandbar
for strays, turning the water
white with their sudden rushes,
their instincts sure as sharks'.
I think these men are brothers
— Manos. Francisco. Fingers
cut and stinging — *Chinga tu madre!*
— shoulders cramping — brothers
in the salt stink and sweat
of hauling and picking. Mullet
are saved; the trash fish tossed
to two pelicans bobbing astern.
And, finally, in the last few
yards of net, a stingray —
a good three feet, wing-tip
to wing-tip, its dark tail
wicked as a cane, is flipped
into the grey-green water,
as the boat sidles and yaws,
its screws barely turning.

"God, is it still alive?"
a woman standing next to me
says to no one in particular.
But there's no way to know
at this distance — what is it?
thirty yards? Then the boat
kicks up a wake and heads
for harbor. The crowd of snow-birds
gathered to watch disperses
slowly, murmuring. No way
to know. Not then. Not now.

1995

AT SEVENTY

Robert Dana

You don't see yourself
in the morning mirror
anymore. And you tell
yourself you're disloyal,
that you have a tin ear,
and can't tell irony
from kvetch. So what?
At seventy, you no longer
expect old friends
to love you, and you're
sick of stories of the past
because they no longer
matter. Nor do
the day-long silences
that sometimes fall on
you like a cool rain.

But you can't stop there.
To get it exactly right,
you have to stand before
the window, before
the great scrim of sunlight
falling through the woods;
the green wall of leaves:
oak, hickory, feathery
hackberry, the wild cherry;
the dogberry fruiting;
darting shadows of birds;
hearing the thick rush of
wild flowers down the damp
slope; tasting the bitter
bite of black, thrice-
boiled, late-morning coffee.

Good luck's your wife's
laughter. And the yellow-
eyed, grey smoke cat,
der Meistersinger, who
keeps a clock in his belly
and knows what time it is.
And your small, muscular,
green-eyed, clouds-on-milk
cat, who seeks, each day
on the living room floor,
the exact center of the universe,
give or take an inch
or two, east or west, north
or south, curling herself
under on it, folding in
her long paws, bouldering in,
as if to mark it clearly,
hold it firmly in place.

MERVEILLE DES QUATRE SAISONS

Robert Dana

Today, I lifted the row
cover, tore up the remains
of some bitter endive and
bug-shot oak leaf lettuce,
and planted three, short
new rows: Merveille des Quatre
Saisons, Loma, and Simpson.
Little brown seed doused
with water and faith. Then,
I took all the remaining
onion sets — the yellow,
the Bermudas with their wine-
colored papers, and dumped
them wholesale into shallow
trenches, thinking, "It's
mid-August. I'll take
what I get." A man doesn't
know what he is until
he kneels on the brown earth,
breaking its damp clods
between his fingers, sifting
it down, spreading a place
level with his hands, carry-
ing it away under his nails.

THE KNOT

Robert Dana

March 21st. One day
after the vernal equinox.
Second day of spring.
Jackstraws of frost
tumble up the glass
of my rented window.
It's six above. Sunny.
But the sun packs
no kick, no heat. And
the little rail lines
of crystals tracking west
across the pane, pinched
and fuzzy, catawampus,
weave the skewed web
of a drugged spider.

My room looks out on
the back of The Church
of Doubting Thomas
where the faithful enter
at odd hours by the back
door, and an iron
starling never flies
from its black perch
above fifty yards
of frozen water hose.

In a small winter-
shattered garden off
to the side, a larger
than life-size Blessed
Virgin prays relent-
lessly, day and night,
a broadsword rising
from between her feet,

upward along her thighs
to a point just below
her breasts; its hilt
strung with a stone
rosary, beads joined
at the crucifix; her
sparrows warming them-
selves in her arbor
and on the shallow stone
abutments of the church.

A man in the blue shirt
and suspendered, dark blue
trousers of Maintenance
opens the door now
and sweeps some dust
and grit onto the bitten,
already dirty snow.
He pays no attention
to the wind whipping
sea-green salt crystals
from the walkway, the
tumbled bird basin,
the cocked lattice where
a dormant vine signs
its wicked Celtic knot.

FIREWORKS

Robert Dana

This is the silver hour.

The sun crowning in the high cusps of the oaks.
Its light spilling down over the cascading leaves.

An elegance old and European.

The trees, all of them —
the oaks, mulberry, dogwoods & wild cherries,
the shagbarks & hackberrys —

from seeds brought here in the pockets of immigrants,
the beaks of birds.

Over the years,
scattering windbreaks, small civilities of shade
across smothering prairie —

a thousand miles of grass
so tall you could tie it across your saddle horn.

*

Frozen stars.

My gin and tonic frets and fizzes in its glass lit by a slice of lemon.

From somewhere, murmurs.

The cries of faraway children.
Neighbors at their Thursday night Bible meeting.

Low highway surf.

Algorithms of what?

*

I've become a lesson.

A poem on the page of a calendar for use in schools.
A list of questions.

Well, that's new.

"Ask students to list places they would write their names."
"Ask 'What means a lot to you?'"
"Ask students 'What color is the spirit?'"

The randomness of simple systems computes to infinite complexity,
we're told.

There's no stopping.
And there are no shortcuts.

All systems must be played out through thousands of generations.

Alive on the breath-edge of metaphor.

Alive in the bird-chat of the sweetness of oncoming evening.
Waiting for the wonder of darkness.

                              *

And in the mornings,
or through the long, heavy, rumpled heat of early summer afternoons,

my shadow cat,
invisible,
            reclining amid the iridescence, the pelluscence of certain roses.

How many generations of randomness to the pattern that ignites

that inner light,
that transparency?

The whole garden exploding like a sky of Chinese fireworks.

*

The elegant lady's gone.
Her intelligence and her decencies.

I saw her dressed impeccably yesterday like a doll of age.
Saw the cover closed gently on her as the cover of a favorite book is closed.

Then, the expensive, polished, perfectly grained oak casket
lowered inside the bronzed, watertight vault
lowered into the minutely turning earth.

A few shovelsful of dirt,
A child's rose.

Sun emerging from behind clouds.

Later, rain.

*

Certainty's a luxury.

Never having had it, I've nothing to teach you.

There's nothing about me
                    of Orpheus, or Augustine, or Jonathan Edwards

on the steps of whose old church
I used to wait for the bus home to Nowheresville.

Even my name's not mine.

It's been a tough hitchhike to here.

A couple of more light-years maybe I'll be ready.

COAL

Frank X. Gaspar

Woke to the sound of anthracite
sliding down the truck's long chute
and ran to the window to see snow
spitting over the heaved walk
and the men hauling the big hods into the shed
with their perfect balance, their leaning shoulders
and jutting hips, quick-stepping, someplace
else to get to, the day going off
to that fossil-midden of days
where we come now to rake and sift,
as we did then in the dark bins
when no one thought to look for us,
when we could disappear among the black sooty
paragons of coal, this in a time before art
and language — only God making us promises,
spreading His truth in the aromatics of kerosene
and the iron rust of axeheads and saws:
Coal-dust in slow galactic drift before
the plain field of the shed window, absolute
equations of time and matter coming down
around our ears and filling the nose and heaping
their bounty upon eyelash and hay-rake,
the quick hearts beating at the edge of winter,
and a sudden voice calling out, sharp as air,
and the moment receding according to all
the scriptures of nature, *once, once,*
the small, pale-knuckled hands rummaging,
rubbing the chinked facets of coal, bringing out
the feathery traces of the long-dead ferns and leaves,
those dim ghosts polished, locked in falling light.

Frank X. Gaspar

Like the surprised angels in Chagall's
rare world, or those dreamy mosaics
of the Divine Constantine,
your feet would scarcely
touch a black paving-stone
if you walked out with me:
you'd float as I
believe I sometimes do
under the wet eaves
of the darkened houses,
down the long halls of the dead
elms, on the last breath
of the foghorns,
coming finally
to the town's watery end,
where we can do nothing
but turn back again
or stand dumb
in the false light, tempted once more
by the old idea that the sea
might stand for something radiant beyond our senses,
or that this land's end might be
a pallid emblem — that our lives
really *are* small things and must be touched
gently or be torn beyond restoring,
like a spotted moth's wing I crushed once
as a child, meaning no harm,
meaning only a kind of homage
to what I know now
is that quality Goethe described,
saying that in everything transitory
is a metaphor for the unknowable.
In this hush, nothing passes.
I can hear a dory chafe
its painter's splice against

a mooring ring, and just
as easily I can judge
how each footfall
that ever raised a summer's dust here
has filed its way among
the mute forms of the vanished trees.
And when you hear the lone
clear note of the struck bell
rising from its buoy,
you will think it prospers
like a strange kind of love,
for we can think of nothing else
to call it, even while it flies to us
over the water, even as it becomes
itself again, clanging its warning,
falling silent.

STEALING

Frank X. Gaspar

Dropped over the fence and rolled
to the side of the house, dark
for nights, the owners gone back
to wherever they go, the drama
of my own stealth so alien
to the world of real people
I wanted to laugh, even as I
slipped beneath the window, felt
its casing with the palm
of my glove, judged against it
and pressed along the shadows to
the cellar door, an inspiration,
cracked it open and crouched down
the steps, penlight on, scoping
the next move in the light's needle:
the second door, moldy, padlocked —
tore away the hasp with the pry-bar
and entered the web-hung cellar,
cold under the rough beams, found
the ladder and trapdoor and rose
hard to a small hallway, smoothing
back the heavy rug over the hatch,
in now, the bulky shapes of furniture
blooming in my night-vision as
I cupped the little light, let its
glow ooze from between my fingers:
Now the search, slow, comfortable,
easy, the town dead in sleep, nothing
to halt this trespass: empty
dresser, stripped bed, medicine
cabinet clean, worthless flatware
in the kitchen drawers, the television
too heavy to lug out of there
on a winter night, some records
I still remember, names

that I would only connect
after years: *Piaf, Vivaldi,*
and in the bookcase a photograph,
two naked men, one's face buried
between the thighs of the other,
something I moved from quickly
but came back to again before

I left with some small things
in my pockets, among them
a silk necktie and a deck of cards:
Then out the side door, nudging
it quietly locked behind,
bending past the brittle hedge
and heading toward the beach
where only the guilty might ever
see me slipping home, not thinking
that someday this might be
a memory I'd try to wake from
saying, *no, that could never
have been me, not me,* but walking
then in the quarter moon, an exuberant
wind on my face, celebrating
how I'd gone out again,
pushed my fingers into
some stranger's heart, and me
the only one to know.

Frank X. Gaspar

Now it is Christmas in the woods
and the pines are hung with gloomy light,
the black silk on the pond's eye
has clouded in its wax of ice,
and two boys that I remember
have come to gather red berries
and the boughs of the white pine,
an idea that no one put them up to
although they talk about their mothers
as though such a thing might make
a happiness around the doors of a house,
as though only the women would know
what to do with an armload of red and green:
And it's my friend and I walking
the corrupt ice of the pond until
we see the purple tangle of the winter-berry bush
and the yellow stalks of the dead reeds
and suddenly his legs burst through
in a great crash and gush—up to his knees
in the shallow water, and he curses
and lumbers to shore, smashing a wake
of splintered ice while I, a few feet away
walk as though charmed. Later, sacks filled
with berries and on a dark hill hacking
the bottom-most tender branches of pine,
we see that his brown pants have frozen
and he bends them, makes them crackle
around the instep of his boot. I don't
have to ask if he is cold. His face is
flushed and young and beautiful,
though I would not have said so then,
but now, refracted across so much memory and longing
it darkens any recollection that might follow it:
I know we must have hiked home in the short

winter dusk with our arms full of garland,
but I don't recall our mothers' greetings
nor can I remember the sprays on the weathered doors
or windowsills, nor the Christmas lights
of that particular year. And the boys,
who have gone forward into the brambles
of what we call lives, are gone forever
except for the persistent traces in one
mind or another, never to be trusted, already
passed into the intricate fiction of what is behind.
Longing for what, then? When the sun
draws behind the low hills west of the pond,
the alder still purples, the winter-dead
grasses still bleach in the bone cold: even
though new houses break the clean lines
of thicket, there is a luster that comes up
in moments before the sky gives over
to the waiting stars: no matter how you watch it,
you cannot gauge the precise moment it vanishes,
you cannot be sure what you wanted to rush to
and gather in your arms and save.

A FIELD GUIDE TO THE HEAVENS

Frank X. Gaspar

Tonight I am speaking in tongues again.
Listen to all the stars with names as old as Mesopotamia:
Rukbat Arkab, Nunki, Lesath, Shaula. They are shining forth
in the Archer and the Scorpion. They are ablaze in the southern sky.
The Scorpion rests his tail on some trees and a streetlight. Now and then
when I go inside to warm some coffee or toast some bread, I read
a few snatches of Milton, who laments death as the loss of intellect,
who says, *Are not the towers of heaven filled with armed watch?*
I am looking for certain signs, certain deliriums. This Scorpion
is the same that stung mighty Orion to death. This Archer
pursues him for all eternity, in his left hand the bow, in his right,
the flaming arrow. This region is rich and manifold. In this direction
lies the center of our galaxy, a holy fire. *Aloof the vulgar constellations thick,*
says Milton, and I walk outside again. The ducks over in the park
are raving mad. Their sounds float on the night wind. The neighbors sleep
in one another's arms. Listen: *Dschubba, Antares, Acrab.* What
are they saying in the aisles and naves of the light years? What
is the sacred word on the street? What celestial music am I
so afraid to miss? In my right hand there is nothing. In my left
hand there is a cup. In my short chair in the shadows I am invisible.
This is how I know my street is a garden and my yard is a bower.
My coffee cools in the slow breeze. Someone's cat circles,
curious, lets me touch the scruff of its neck before it goes off to hunt
for meat or sex. The shrubs and trees and flowers all become
one another's equals in the slow eyes of darkness. *Sing,*
heavenly Muse, says Milton. *Geidi, Nashira, Dabih.* Eat
every fruit, sleep soundly: surely, verily, nothing will be lost.

HOBBES

Frank X. Gaspar

For he can leap, but he doesn't bother with that too much —
mostly he sleeps or chatters in the windows at birds out on
the wires. I maintain that he is worthless, some misbegotten
kin to a possum, and in fact he came from a bad litter, a bad
neighborhood. There's something not right about him. How
then to name him *Hobbes*, as my son did, though I lobbied for
Meatloaf? We have an understanding. I don't make Hobbes out to be
more than he is, which just is some wild thing with an impossibly
tiny brain and no morals. For his part, he ignores me unless he
thinks I have food. I enjoy the purity of this contract, for it guides
me in my dealings with humans, which are few, at any rate, but
without much surprise or disappointment now that I've learned
not to expect others to be better than I am myself, now that I've
stopped raging at everyone else's smallness. We get what we
deserve, mostly. I won't say I learned this from a cat, I won't
try to make a tidy moral — nothing sweet or cloying. For he can
entertain himself by staring at the wall or licking his body parts,
which acts afford him great pleasure and from which I can derive no
honest instruction. And he brings grief and terror to the household
spiders, whom I have always liked and so he places me in an
unsupportable position, a soft neutrality which ensures peace in
no corner, justice for none but the strong. My dream is to one day
be young and strong and garlanded with justice. Let the dead bury
the dead, let the sparrows and starlings compose their conga-lines
out on the boughs and conduits — it just might *be* a world without end,
feral and imperfect, though I admit I want to own it, I want to touch it,
I want to curl up in it and sleep in it forever, as though I am loved for
something beyond my control or choosing, as though even the dust
over my eye is what I am dreaming and I know exactly what it means.

THE HOLYOKE

Frank X. Gaspar

The raised iron letters,
those two words stamped in an arc
on that old water-heater in the bathroom,
The Holyoke,
are the first symbols that I ever unraveled,
my great-uncle telling me their sound,
pulling the e in The out long
like the whistle of a teakettle.

The heater didn't work.
We heated our water stovetop
in a copper tub, unremarkable,
but a fact I cling to
as I cling to the quality of light
that seemed always spread
over the tight sidewalk along the house,
a winter gray, old ice, coal ash,
the film over my great-uncle's eye.

When my great-uncle died
his pension stopped coming.
That was the bad time.
Some while after that I got curious.
I opened the arched door
of the old heater
and stared at a helix of coils
thick with dust.
I spent the day there
on the bathroom floor,
measuring my way to the heart of the thing,
turning pipes,
reaming fixtures with an old coathanger.

When I was through I filled the kerosene bottle
and lighted the wick.
Dusk came on, and that flat light
hung in the square window.
When I opened the faucet, water came,
staccato, brown, warm as flesh.

IT IS THE NATURE OF THE WING

Frank X. Gaspar

The problem is being a fragment trying to live out a whole life.
From this, everything follows. Or the problem is being
fractured and preoccupied with one's own mending, which
lasts as long as you do and comes with its legion of distractions.
Just now, when a lovely-throated motor comes gliding up
the street to one driveway or another, I can tell you
there is a certain kind of safety in a fact like that. It is so
solid you can lean on it in your bad hours. It can lift you, too,
from your despair, which is of no consequence, which can
be measured against the dropping flowers of the wisteria,
which fall because of their nature and essence, and stain
the redwood planks of the small deck in the back of the house.
That doesn't mean those used-up blossoms feel at home
under everyone's feet or at the mercy of my stiffened broom.
Didn't Plato say it is the nature of the wing to lift what is heavy?
He was speaking of love again, I can remember that much, and
then love was a ladder, too, but lifting again, always upward.
Then it is possible to love Plato for his faith, which is so strong
he becomes difficult and obdurate in the late nights. He is
hardly distracted by a passing car. He is fixed on something
beautiful, and why not? When I step out onto the porch, there
is nothing shining in the sky. Oh, and the wisteria blooms have
fallen some more and are like a sad carpet. And some small
insects are dancing in the garage's yellow lamp. They don't hear
the little bats squeaking. It's all right. You could even say they
look happy, they look joyful. Surely they are beautiful in their
ignorance and danger. See how they hold your head and command
your eye? Looking upward? Looking toward that homely light?

THE INVENTION OF POINTILLISM

Steve Gehrke

Once, in the apartment of a woman I barely knew,
　　　　in a room made of blurred light and ashes
with carpet the color of very old newspaper,
　　　　I began to believe love was a collection of sighs
and small gestures that flew off as we moved.

　　　　I was foolish and romantic. I didn't know
that the sound of her children, splashing in the pool
　　　　outside her bedroom window, that the tips
of her husband's shoes aimed at me
　　　　from the closet, that even the print of Seurat's

The Circus, hung at an angle near the bed
　　　　would never leave me. Afterward, I stood
in her bathroom, watching a face (barely my own),
　　　　waver in my hand's cupped water,
not knowing that each cell remembers desire

　　　　the way each shard of the bottle shattered on the asphalt
outside her apartment remembered thirst,
　　　　the way the bones of the finch that lay next to the bottle,
equally shattered, remembered flight. I believed,
　　　　at climax, that each cell was thinking

one thought, or not thinking at all, but opening
　　　　like a tiny mouth to release its fraction of the soul.
I didn't know this meant I could never leave that
　　　　room. Do you see? Even now, I am that woman,
drawn and re-drawn in the light below the window,

　　　　I am the water crashing over the edge of the pool,
the darkness gathering in the bottom of the shoes,
　　　　in the spaces between the threads of the carpet.
I can even be the children, doing as they are told,
　　　　choreographing, for the sake of the father,

their lies, like flashlights aimed at the night sky
            to re-create the moon. Do you see? I can be anything
in that room. Except, perhaps, for the husband.
            But if, some mornings, he sits with the paper,
pretending to read, but really watching his family orbit

            through the V of light as he turns the pages, as he believes,
stubbornly, in their goodness, what could
            be wrong with that? And if he wakes
some nights, driven from that place where he sleeps
            with only a small road of bed between him and his wife,

 if he stands, suddenly, to adjust the picture on the wall,
            if he places one foot then the other onto carpet
the color of news that doesn't matter anymore, and stares
            into the face of each painted dot, which at this hour of night
would be clotted with darkness, and if he thinks

            not of the ballerina's foot slipping from the side of the horse,
the body of the tumbler bent grotesquely and disjointed,
            if instead he thinks, briefly and not for the first time,
the only truth is the truth within a single cell, even I will
            be forced to believe him. Do you see? We have

only two choices. We can believe, stubbornly, that the picture
            on the wall is whole. Or we can imagine
Seurat, as a boy, holding a fresh brush in his hand,
            thinking, "I will show them how easily
they are tricked," then narrowing the tip with his mouth.

FIRST SNOW: A MEMORY

Steve Gehrke

During filming, Fred Astaire insisted on so many takes that Ginger Roger's shoes turned pink with blood.
— American Encyclopedia of Film

I'm watching a movie with my grandfather
        who tells me that the snow outside
is the word of God, translated into the intricate
        alphabet of the infinite, "like Chinese
characters," he says, so that I turn to listen
        to each flake extinguishing itself
against the window, and he turns himself
        so completely into his own breathing
that I'm sure, for him, sleep is a hiding place,
        a kind of prayer, the snow encasing
his armchair, muffling even the movie.

        Which I remember now only as a vague
black-and-white, but which made an impression
        so strong that some days, when it snows,
I think of Fred Astaire, knocking loose chips
        of plaster from a ceiling so poorly made
it sometimes crumbles on its own. Or I call
        each flake a discarded note from music
that evaporates as it plays, as Fred tries
        to erase each of Ginger's moves,
to thread them beneath the shadows of his own.

Which is how, from above, we must appear,
        trying to thread our particular kind of music
into the landscape, the music of not-having-
        anywhere-else-to-go, the tune an exhausted
traveler whistles, not to keep himself awake,
        but to bind himself to the emptiness,
making a vacancy inside each note
        where he can curl up and fall asleep.

Years ago, as I was watching the glass
        murder each flake of snow,
my grandfather woke to tell me that, in the end,
        Fred Astaire, defeated from a hundred
takes, collapsed at Ginger's bloody feet.
        I was too young to sense, until now,
what he wanted me to learn: we ruin beauty
        so we can pray for its return.

SHINGLES

Steve Gehrke

Today, my grandfather's muscles are an answer
to the blizzard that battered and tore the shingles
from his roof, an answer to the wind that tries
and tries to lift his shadow from the wood.

He pounds each new shingle into place,
as if to say, *there, you won't be doing that again.*
His hammering startles birds from the ledge,
but can't drown out his off-key singing:

  the work, the working, just the working life …

His voice travels through the eaves, onto the splash-
block, into the lawn and below the grass
where it is 1923, and a late-April storm keeps
his father from the fields, sending him from room

to room, whistling and flipping his pocket-
watch open and closed, his boredom warming
into lust, on the day his eleventh child, my grandfather,
is conceived. On the sofa, my great-grandmother

shuffles the cards for a game of Crazy Eight,
her hands deep in habit, her mouth hot from scolding
the children. By now, even her thoughts
are small children, scurrying, bold and un-chaperoned,

through her mind, locking themselves into tiny rooms
and giggling. When he comes to her,
when he sends the boys out to shovel the long drive
and leads her to the bed, unbuckling the tops

of his overalls on the way, she thinks of herself
as the snow, swooning and drifting against the side
of the house. The storm mounts and mounts
inside her, the snow fusing into my grandfather's

bones, the wind slipping between each flake
to become his singing. Now, that snow melts
into the sweat at the back of his neck,
the saliva building and receding in his mouth.

If he thinks of his mother at all, if he hears her
in the soft cry each bent and rusted nail makes
when he yanks it from the wood, it doesn't interfere
with his work. He will strike the last nail

long past exhaustion, his shoulders tight
from swinging the hammer, his throat closing
around its thirst, even as he carries his song
into the lawn, his voice drifting and swooning —

> *out with the old, and in with the new*
> *lost my hat and replaced it with a shoe ...*

The weathered shingles lie scattered near
the edge of the house, some of them
like tiny shut doors to the past, others
flipped open and open by the wind.

The last thing she said to him was, "Climb up
to the roof and see if you can get rid
of that awful sun." Years from now, when
nearly every day from his childhood

has fallen to the floor of his memory
and shattered, he will think of the storm
his mother told him of, he will think it is best
to die, not in your sleep, but in a wind

so fierce it swoops you in and drags you
back to the moment when the odds
against your birth crumbled, the first cry,
not yours, but your mother's, her legs

raised in a rehearsal of labor. How else
would you know that even the worst
of your history was a series of conquests?
How else would you know that you had won?

Steve Gehrke

> *Honor a going thing.*
> — *A.R. Ammons (1926-2001)*

Wind across the bay this morning, the way thought alters
the texture of the brain. Up-shore, a man sleuths the dunes,
walking his metal detector like a pet, calling forth the trinkets
from the sand. He cannot know that from where I stand —
the tide revising its shadow at my feet — I test his surface
for some scrap of you:
                           your morning stride, sun like concentration,
your vision braided, again, into questioning: not encroaching,
not encoding, just releasing, like homing pigeons, your intellect
across the chemistries: a mobile of gulls hanging over the waves,
the minnows' atmospheric swirl, beach plum, pitch, the ocean's
deepest cells ascending, like buckets drawn from the darkness
of wells: the whole surf caught in the downdraft of your listening.
Honor the gone world,
                           the glistening ruins just below our feet:
lost keys, rings, foil off a stick of gum, the rusted shards
like coal dust in the lungs. Everywhere words are partial
and complete: they bind and unbind, like a magician's rings,
like atoms finding, continually, the angles of release.
They liberate the shore, and all day the man in which we meet,
guided by the signals that pulse through the sand
like whale-song through the waves, bows down to rescue the debris.

ABHIJAT ASKS: WHY DO WE EXIST?

Steve Gehrke

If there is only one world,
it is the world of the mind.

And tonight my mind feels like a football
stadium, where all the fans are heading

for the exits. I can almost hear them clattering
down the narrow stairwell of my spine,

clicking through the interlocking
cross-walks of logic, the light

switching back and forth:
Exist   Don't Exist   Exist

If there is only one language,
it starts with the brain's own loneliness.

And tonight, it feels like the intricate
grooves and bulges on my brain

are a sketch for a personal heaven
abandoned before construction

could begin, before even
the first board was nailed.

If we die only once, it takes
a very long time, atom by atom,

each thought killing off the last.
I think we exist because we can't

not exist, because the mind
is a neighborhood where all night

one tiny house darkens,
just as another fills with light.

LAKE LAFAYETTE

Sam Harrison

Tannin makes the water
The color of half-brewed coffee
Where it stands up under the bony
Arch of the cypress knees.
The water is still, there,
Enclosed in the shadow
The tree lets down
On the surface.
In it there is no time,
No breeze,
No thinking,
No movement but the
Outrageously slow
Pulsing of something
Behind it.

In it there are fish.

On the horizon
The cypress wrap
Like torn ribbon,
Weaving through channels
We dont see,
Fluttering —
The border
For quick-sketch clouds
Boring through
In ragged lines
Like driven elephants
Trumpeting worlds
Without sound.

We came for the fish.

We knew the train would come.
Fishing down the embankment,
Water on both sides of the track,
We crossed to the side the truck was on
In case it was a long one.
And when it had passed,
When the steel wound
Pounded elsewhere in the marsh,
The cypress pool's ancient body
Carried on its tongue

The swirl of the fish.

THE MEANING OF BOILED PEANUTS

Sam Harrison

The half-learned sound
Of wind in dry leaves, sustained
And remote overhead;
The air, warmed by a lean sun
But smelling cold;
An open patch of ground
Where men's feet
Had left the hard clay head
Of the earth shining —

A large pot of peanuts
Hangs above a stunted fire
Where two black men and I
Crouch wordless with our whiskey,
Sucking down the dancing vapors.

THE VILLAGE

Sam Harrison

Near the aluminum gate
Where Wadesborough road
Becomes open pasture,
On a small rise
Of thinned pines

Stand six decayed streetcars
With delicately arched
Wooden roofs
And painted numbers
Flaked from sides.

Rusted metal grates
Lock glassless windows
To nothing. Flowering
Weeds trail
Through crumbled steel.

Several tin extensions
Form roofs
Enclosing cool
Squares of dirt.
In one is a mattress.

I had my picture taken
In a vestibule
To send to friends
In the north
Who rent.

SPELL FOR A POET GETTING ON

Lola Haskins

May your hipbones never die.
May you hear the ruckus of mountains
in the Kansas of your age, and when
you go deaf, may you go wildly deaf.

May the neighbors arrive, bringing entire aviaries.
When the last of your hair is gone, may families
lovelier than you can guess colonize
the balds of your head.

May your thumbstick grow leaves.
May the nipples of your breasts drip wine.
And when, leaning into the grass, you watch
the inky sun vanish into the flat page

of the sea, may you join your lawn chair,
each of you content
that nothing is wise forever.

Lola Haskins

For the daffodil's horn that blazes spring For the hooting taxis
that don't give a damn whose door they crunch For the Levis
of New York City, out at the knees

For the shadows between hardwoods that hint of zebras For
the zebra's yellow teeth that will bite if she can For the way
her stripey neck can twist itself towards your arm For other
beauties: the peacock and his unpleasant voice

For vivid violet lightning that won't stay put For the sound
thunder makes after love, the bang that makes you jump
no matter how you steel, no matter how you want the flash
to be enough

For the jittery innocence under the skins of rivers the clear
way they skip over rocks as though the rocks' indigestibility
were of no importance For the stones women swallow
when they marry For the operation that removes the stones
so they can be kept as specimens or set in rings

For the way the birds do not realize they are flying For
the baby who hums himself awake For the cat in her
orange disregard For the moment just before we understand
what the promised little talk is all about

THE RIM BENDERS

Lola Haskins

*Perhaps the most critical moment in the construction of a grand piano is
that in which the strip of wood which will be the final casing of the
instrument must be matched to the curve of the frame.*

They have twelve minutes to marry
the thin edge to its curve.
There is great pressure. Fine wood
does not wish to bend. Let us
lean with them into this poem.

And if we fail, the set glue
leaves gaps, sharp mistakes
of air we will always see.
But how can we not try? These are
the twelve minutes of our lives.

Lola Haskins

For years I made you purple presents.
Mauve blouses, lavender skirts,
fuschia scarves that flowed.
For each occasion, another shade
of bruise, sweet as the fumes of
Daddy's disappearing Buick, achy as
the strokes of tight-lipped Mommy,
brushing my hair. I thought you'd
wear them. I thought they'd become
you, being blonde. But you put them,
all my purple gifts, in one deep drawer.
And now, grown, you take them out.
At first it pains, how new they are.
Then you smile. *Let's give these*
away, you say. And the spring sun
backlights your hair. You look
like some kind of angel, standing
there in your bedroom, the shine
of what to keep, and what to let go
falling through both our hands.

DJANGO IN HANG-ZHOU

Lola Haskins

He is *waiguo ren*: foreigner. When he walks to
the market his dark head sees over theirs as if
he were a child, held on his father's shoulders.
They point at him and stare. He is twenty-one,
and empty as a thousand year-old wine jug.
He is also in love, not with what is foreign
in Hang-Zhou, but with what is most himself —
the cold and ancient lake, the blue mountains,
and, in spring, with the puffs of dust that followed
the galloping carts of emperors. I think he was
among the watchers who lined the streets when
these trees were small. I asked him once,
Why is it that Mandarin's so easy for you?
Because I'm a musician, he said, which was
like the doll, that still has many dolls inside.

THE .38

Lola Haskins

for H.P. (1943-1962)

The first time you unlocked your glove compartment and showed me
your secret, I was breathless at what nestled in its box like jewelry.
Then, slowly, I grew used to what rode with us, and on clear days,

when we'd drive to the beach, I came to understand it preferred
its double dark to our light, where you were touching my breasts
under my shirt. And as we began to think more and more about

our natures (you saw me as glitter flaked off schist, to me you were
the gesso angel that brought the annunciation), I decided I was not
sorry you kept it in your car, just there, not for anything. Until

the March afternoon you took it out, laid it across your hand,
and said *Have I told you I have bullets?* Then the .38 turned rattler
across my path, and jealousy crept into me and I wanted it gone.

So you put it away, and it went back to sleep. And one midnight,
as we were heading home, south on 101, lights all around us, as if
we had been sent to the sky, I felt my nipple diminish as it

tightened, and I thought, because this was my first time, *Yes,
I will marry you.* But I didn't say it. So you had to pull up to
my parents' house in your red Mercedes that summer evening

and demand, *Come now.* But my parents and I were leaving.
You drove off, washed in the scent of gardenias at the top of
our garden. The rest of this is for the .38, because even

your ashes are forty now, and I don't think you're listening.
I'm sorry, .38. I was wrong. It wasn't you he craved after all.
It was the featherless bird he became when he stepped off the rail.

And all the way down to the steel water, he must have been happy
as he never was. Oh .38, he has left us both. You were his sister,
his mother, his charm. You kept him safe as long as you could.

Lola Haskins

The parking lots of K-Mart are not safe. There are video cameras on school buses, and metal detectors in the halls of universities. Every time she gives an F she feels something burn into the back of her neck.

When the telephone rings again at three a.m. with breathing and you startle awake, you know the police can do nothing, unless afterwards. The chain rattling at your entry cannot kill you. So you tell yourself, as you dial 911, the believer's number.

Elsewhere, food sent to starving Somalis is sold in little heaps on the street: rice, flour, the dry powder that is milk. In Bosnia, children are born already raped. Their mothers do not know any more what to love.

There is a man held in the dark. He is not allowed to speak. One day, the chatter of the guards, record played backwards, fades out. At the man's door a poem softly knocks. He memorizes it. The poem is his charm, his small control. It is how he stays alive.

Lola Haskins

Each drop of sea contains
all the fish that have ever lived,
each grit of sand the heart
of all the rocks that have risen
above the land or laid upon it.

When Ava who is ten days old today
cries, and I sing her the lullaby
that makes her head go soft against
my shoulder, she is every old woman
who has ever fallen asleep.

THE SAND HILL CRANES

Lola Haskins

The blue air fills with cries of regret.
The cranes are streams, rivers.
They danced on the night prairie,
leapt at each other, quivering.

The long bones of sand hill cranes
know their next pond. Not us.
When something is too beautiful,
we do not understand to leave.

Janet Holmes

The first Mary was stolen, so now Our Lady
prays behind bars outside the Nambé Church, her *nicho*
lit like a small stadium. The church's hill
affords a view of the mountains appropriately scenic,
but I took you behind it to look straight up in darkness
at August's meteors, shielding the Virgin's klieg
with adobe.

    Well, citydweller, you weren't prepared
for an unlit sky in this bare country, no streetlights
reflecting up to clouds, a clear space
so filled up with stars
it seemed theoretical: what *might* exist out there
if we could see —

      you reminded me
of myself, sixth grade, learning constellations
with Randy Konigsberg out on my front lawn,
California beneath our backs, head to head,
the astrochart passing between us. Even that young,
my thoughts slid down to where I was (*what if
he and I ...*)

      as, behind the church, neck craned back,
what if, I thought again ...

       as if the universe,
brought home as more than bright small points
attractively arranged, forced people closer together
for something like protection, to keep them
from flying off the planet toward something
with more pull. I wanted to hold on,

       and you
seemed so much more concrete
than anything else — mudwalled church, stone saint,
earth —

The Milky Way stretched over us like a sea,
and everywhere the random stars made pictures,
heroes and bears that look (on a chart) like
geometric proofs
                        and (in the sky) like fireflies,
meteors shooting through trying to prove
there's life out there, there's movement,
though you can tell that you're alone,
and I didn't reach out, but waited to fall in …

THE LOVE OF THE FLESH

Janet Holmes

Reality is not limited to the tactile:
still, we touch our own faces, as if by the slide
of fingers over cheekbones, eyelids, lips,

we can check that we are not dreaming. This is
the life of the body, the life of gesture,

tangible, a palm against the skin.
When I put my hand to your face it becomes a caress,
but here, against my own, it is disbelief
or wonder.

The questions are hard, as when medieval scholars
divvied up the body in debate
as to where the soul hung its ephemeral hat —

and those who plumped for the heart laboring its fenced-in field
shouted down those others who felt God's messages
precisely in the pit of the stomach,

while the ancients reasoned *the brain, the unromantic brain,*
and virtually every organ had its champion ...

Their filigree of argument confounds me
just as, then,
the suddenness of love left me dazed:

for days they had to call me twice
to get a single answer — I was deaf
and breathless and stunned. It was not
as if the world were new and beautiful.

It was, instead, as if I had unlearned
how to use my hands
and feet. Where does the life of the body

leave off, the life of the spirit start? When
does the mouthful of air move beyond breathing
towards magic? We made

a spectacle of ourselves, dancing about
like clowns in huge shoes, goofy with happiness,
inarticulate in all but the lexicon
of sexual flesh;

and the soul, from its short-leased home
among the muscles, sent its respects,
or so we were told ...

Even in *Paradise*, the light-filled spirits
long for their resurrection,
and Dante is surprised that they miss their bodies:

"Not only for themselves," he speculates,
"but for their mothers and fathers, and for the others
dear to them on earth,"

souls wistful for flesh, nostalgic
for their faraway, simple selves who walked about

and who, lifting and seeing their hands,
thought suddenly one day *These touch, caress, stroke;*
who found in the body a bridge beyond it

and coined the word *beloved*. And thus we performed
for ourselves the seamless changing over
of element to element,

body to air, solid to spirit, magic trick
or miracle, without knowing the particular
spell or prayer or luck that made it quicken.

Janet Holmes

For two weeks in the summer, she goes every morning
to water the plants at her friend's house, feed the fish,
collect the mail and the papers. Her friend
vacations in New York State, but here
the day is already hazy and full of glare, the damp
steady sort of heat that hits at dawn
and stays. The woman's glad of this little chore.
Unlocking the empty house, she listens: her heels
echo among the rooms. The fish — mostly inch-long brightnesses
called neons — dart to the floating, brittle flakes
she gives them. She turns the geraniums inward,
away from the window, and mists the fern.
The woman is calm, as if at an oasis
where her new job and odd new single life
are of no consequence; her ex-husband
will not call her here to explain again
his reasons for leaving; she will not have to learn
names of new people, or new procedures
in an unfamiliar office.

Now she passes through the other rooms
like a wing or fin, barely disturbing the air,
then locks the front door and tests to see that it's latched.
It's seven-thirty, but already her face
has a tight mask of sweat, and her blouse, gone limp,
has lost its pleats and the crisp, sweet smell of the iron.
The next day, tapping fish food into the water,
she sees on the floor to the left of the tank
a neon, dead. A slight
decaying odor reaches her: she wasn't aware,
at first, but now it seems quite strong, as if
a larger thing had died. All its orange
has faded to putty — she hates to touch it,
but scoops it up in a tissue, quickly flushes.
Then cracks a window, though there's no breeze;

heat continues to weigh on the town
like a judgment in the green shade of the street,
and it seems unlucky to start the morning with burial.

Things get worse, and next day
there's another on the floor, its gray eye
filmed with gel, and after that another.
The woman watches the tank, as if a clue
could be found in the gentle rhythms of fish,
but they seem imperturbable. When, sometimes,
she finds the house as she'd left it, the woman feels
relief, or the lifting-off of sadness, and remembers
her own unhappiness again. But three
or four times more a fish out of water
makes her wonder if there isn't, somehow, something
she doesn't know she's doing wrong. Her friend returns,
and the woman tells this story with an undertone of apology.

It seems there's an explanation. A fighting fish
she hadn't known about, that her friend had thought
was sluggish or sick, had suddenly come to life
and would sometimes chase the others
until, swimming in terror, they flipped themselves
right out of the aquarium. A simple adjustment:
the fighting fish gets moved to a tank of its own.
The woman wants to laugh with relief,
to tell her friend she thought the fish were suicides
and she somehow responsible; but now she's embarrassed
and stays quiet. Instead, she and her friend
set up the barbecue and open all the mail.

Long into the starless heavy night
they sit outside, talking in low voices, and the day's heat lifts
just slightly to a small accompaniment
of wind chimes and silverware. When it's time, the woman
walks back home alone, among the streetlamps
and isolated windows shedding light,
and what she walks through isn't the neighborhood darkness,
common enough — but the swimming thrill
of circles, the question of where to leap.

CELEBRATION ON THE PLANET MARS

Janet Holmes

Music develops what I call a satellite, or orbital, effect.
It keeps going round and round in your mind ...
— Raymond Scott

I. In His Mind's Ear

The six of them, his Quintette: Raymond Scott
surveys his sidemen from the piano as Ptolemy
plotted the moon and planets and sun
around his dominant Earth;

      and it's sphere music for sure he's set them spinning.
Where there's no sound
close to the one he needs, he directs the trumpeter
to dunk his bell in a bucket, playing the water,
the anodized pail, a muted echo of what's
in his mind's ear
because the time he's ahead of drags and drags.
Here's the missionary burbling in the cauldron,
warbling "Dinner Music
for a Pack of Hungry Cannibals."
Nothing you've heard before.
A seduction of sounds. He wants to lure them
down out of the galaxies, into the listening air.
He will lay for them mechanical traps, tempt them
into giving up their names: but for now
he calls the water to work for him simply,
as if it were breath.

II. "Celebration on the Planet Mars"

On the planet Mars they're dancing again,
swinging to jazzy sax in the red, discordant atmosphere,
and at the New York Aquarium
the penguins are swaying in their cage

as a writer for *down beat* — "The tenor sax solos
appeared to have the greatest effect on the birds"—
plays them "The Penguin" and solemnly
observes. The penguins spread their ineffectual wings,
spin uneven circles. They couldn't explain themselves
even if they could speak,
        like the revelers on the red planet
who think of this music as "otherworldly,"
but from what other world? Sirenic, it compels them
forward, as one is compelled to do something foolish
or something new, toward
a kind of bravery.

III. Orbital Effect

Shirley Temple taps with Bill Robinson
in a screening room, in an endless
film loop; the cartoon rabbit
barrels along to "Powerhouse," outwitting the dumb hunter
another million times ...
You can't stop humming.
Each time it's new:
endorphin tunes.
"I want to write music people would like
the first time they heard it," he said, knowing
that then people would never stop
hearing it.

IV. The Jazz Laboratory

He wants to lure them down out of the galaxies,
those elusive reverberations — had meant
to be training his ears to the ether all along,
high school radio wonk turned composer. He wants
an expansion of the lexicon of sound:

how else to set an accompaniment
to the lightspeed future? One needs
new notes, language soldered together
bit by bit in a jazz laboratory,
shot through with electric current
to see whether it breathes by itself. Karloff,
he names it, a machine that sizzles
convincingly as bacon, or wheezes like an asthmatic;
but to build his Clavivox he must use
some of its innards;
the result, a machine that sings
with a human voice, eery
as ectoplasm. In time,
it too gives up its fabricated life:
first to the Videola, then to synthesizers,
sequencers, a scanning radio, even
a serial doorbell;
today, only the Electronium
survives. The man
never applied for a single patent,
who had thirty-two feet of equipment
crowding his workshop,
the lights blinking Mardi Gras
in the artificial heat.
The Electronium cannot, he said, be used
to perform existing music.
It is designed for the instantaneous
composition-performance
of music heard only once,
then left to echo
in its solitary orbit ...

V. "Dedicatory Piece to the Crew and Passengers
    of the First Experimental Rocket Express to the Moon"

In the future, he said, the composer
will sit alone on the concert stage
and merely *think*
his idealized conception of his music
which will be channeled
directly into the minds of his hearers,
allowing for no distortion.
In this way would the seduction be complete:
sounds so compliant as to dance themselves
into the heads of an audience, without
the duenna of technology to mediate ...
no saxophone, no keyboard. All body.
Human.
Come down, one says
to the symphony in the ether.
Be heard.

KINDNESS AT ICHANG

David Kirby

... Ichang, where they shipped the night soil from Chungking.

No one stays here long.
Even the Jesus men stopped coming.
But one of them said before he left forever
that the world wouldn't end in fire
or waves but in great acts of kindness,
and as he spoke I saw above his head
a cloud of dust in which the men of Chungking
danced to the sound of gong and triangle.
They took our rakes and crusty rags,
they bathed us, gave us almond cakes
and wine. A woman rubbed sweet oil
into my skin, a child called me Father,
music rose around me like warm perfume,
but I only heard the soil falling.
only saw the ships upon the river.
The sun glowed like an orange
and I longed for nights in Ichang,
the smell of sulfur, home.

THE WHALE TOTEM

Think of all the prominent
    people who

have lived in that belly:
    surely it

is warm and dry there
    and nicely

furnished. On the other hand.
    the same

dumb jaw that cradled Jonah
    and Pinocchio

closed forever on unbelieving Ahab's
    limb: like

all gods he is generous
    and hungry.

THE OPERA LOVER

David Kirby

Even though the music is still raging,
I have you home already
and out of your clothes.
You are willing but cautious
and wonder what to expect.
Back at the concert hall,
our friends are puzzled
by the suddenly empty seats.

Meanwhile you have decided
to put on a brave front
and go along with the gag;
you smile and raise your arms
and move your feet
to the faraway music.
I'm talking like a crazy person now,
a treasure-mad dwarf
from some German myth
begging you for everything.

David Kirby

Running down the Via degli Annibaldi
I hear Aretha say
my momma said leave you alone
and as I hurry up the steps
of the church of San Pietro in Vincoli
I hear her say my daddy said come on home
and as I turn to go down the right aisle
she says my doctor said take it easy
and then I stop right in front
of Michelangelo's *Moses:*
oh but your loving is much too strong
for these chain chain chains
which were used to bind St. Peter in Palestine
and are themselves preserved under glass
in the same church. Moses is angry;
he's just seen the Israelites
dancing around the Golden Calf
and now he twists his beard with his right hand
and shifts his weight to the ball of his left foot
so he can jump up and smash the stone tablets
with the Ten Commandments on them.

I'd like to be that angry just once —
or, like Bernini's St. Teresa,
to pass out from pleasure! I think of Bo Diddley
as I scurry down the Via XX Settembre
and up the steps of the church of Santa Maria della Vittoria
with its great Baroque sculpture
in which the angel smiles at the saint
as sweetly as a child would, yet his copper arrow
is aimed between her legs;
God might as well have told Teresa
he walked forty-seven miles of barbed wire,
got a cobra snake for a necktie

and a house by the roadside made out of rattlesnake hide
because, really, the only question is,
Who do you love?

THE PHYSICS OF HEAVEN

David Kirby

Everyone will be there at once:
your husbands and boyfriends
in their relation to you

as the wife and sweetheart of each
but also in equivalent if not identical relationships
with their other wives and sweethearts:

Harry, Edward and Maurice will coexist peacefully
with themselves and with you
but also with Sheila, Nancy, Kim, and so on,

and all at the same time. And you, you'll be all
your happy selves: a little girl, a big girl, a woman,
a baby, everything except dead. And the pets!

Here's Beowulf, who died under the wheels of a milk truck,
running and playing again! And Matilda, who chased you
around the porch when she had distemper,

wagging her tail now as she licks your hand.
And all the fish who died before you could give them names,
though you meant to. And both hamsters.

And your parents, but this time they love each other,
which is to say they love themselves, love you.
It doesn't make sense. But no one notices, so it makes sense.

David Kirby

No one you want to be here, is —
but the boy you invited to your twelfth birthday,
the one who called you that morning

and said he had a cold, even though
everyone else had seen him the night before
at the football game, running and laughing,

he's here — you were the only one without a date
at your own party because he wasn't there,
but he's here, smirking, empty-handed.

And the others, all the guys you'd broken up with,
they're here, too, with all the other girls
they've shamed and maddened, quarreling,

the din unbearable. It's the worst of times
and the worst of times. The friends who bored you
and then broke with you because you weren't interesting

are here, and so are the pets you starved,
the ones you let run in the street,
whose tails you pinched in the doors of their cages.

And you, you act selfish, break hearts —
you do what everyone else does, because hell makes sense.
But no one notices, so it doesn't make sense.

Judith Kitchen

Yesterday the clouds were flat
and heavy with snow. Now
they have lifted. What luck,
this morning, driving east

into the sun, that the boy
on the corner of Culver and Main
exhales, a visible pouring out
of breath so tangible

it *is* a halo. Ice is stronger
than grief, casting back
the sun like Christmas tinsel.
Each puddle flares and instant

as I pass. Cold is a kind of
purity; the lungs run clear,
fill the body with their small
subverted wings. Yes, winter

is coming, it's in the air,
in the sound of my boots
on the pavement. Paw prints,
locked in cement, glint

as though an animal, freed
of the need to be itself,
had skimmed the night. Wherever
you are, I wanted to tell you.

LARGO

Judith Kitchen

Outside my window, nothing but snow.
It recedes in increments, tattered skirts

on the lawn. What we feel in morning air
is breathlessness — an intake of light

that is held, like the high note in a choir.
You say you have flowers, irises waving.

How can I enter your spring? The clock
at noon aligns its hands, and outside

the window there are branches. Birds wing in
as if they were the ones forsaken. Snow

is edged with light. Breathless, I branch
into my loss, taking the song for granted.

WINTER LANDSCAPE

Judith Kitchen

Beyond the rail fence, horses
stand nose to the wind. They might
as well be statues. Everywhere,

everywhere we look, trees weld earth
to a flat white sky. The car
moves between these walls of white,

accepting the vagaries of wind,
drifts that swirl in to catch us up
in moments of forgetfulness.

Let us believe the impossible. Let us
slide between two griefs so easily
they seem remote as history. This

is the meaning of white — a day
so cold, so undemanding, that the
heart itself lies briefly still.

for Judson

This is where our lives intersect, here
on the surface of this lake, flat stones arcing
and skittering along the top

in a calculus of their own. Yes, our summers
have come together — the tomboy in me rising
like yeast, and the dream of Triple A hot

in your bent arm, driving its curve and
sudden snap. Who would believe we would come
to watch stones skim along the glass

as though madness could not rise in each of us?
Live your life, you say, *without looking
for the poem.* And *yes,* I say, *we used shale,*

*flatter than any rock you southern boys
have handled.* Yes, I say, this is the record —
clear-headed hops that flatten out, resist

the water, ride on its tension. Whatever we were
we are now. All those words stored up
to spill across the page, all those

half-spent days we want to call "experience."
You must have been quite young those summers
I rode the convertible, feet on the dash,

long hair spilling to the wind. How old was I
when you clutched the ball, wound
your arms back, let it fly toward home plate?

So how do we know what is truth, except
by the way we each have reached down, pried
a rock from the bank, let it fly out

over the air before it sinks into memory?
Saturday, late August, rain a slow drizzle
that makes a sheen on the highway. I do not

think of you, but the stones, heaped somewhere
at the bottom of a lake, finding a place
where what has gone will not matter.

It matters though. One moment overlays
another until we never are quite sure
which way it went, or when it disappeared.

Judith Kitchen

As if the mind could choose
what to recall. As if summer spread
at the back of the brain,
yellow petals drifting down
from the garage wall. One scent
and your bodies were hard
on the grass. Touch me, he said,
and you did, though
that is not really the story.

As if the body could be more
than a set of patterns.
More than a child who needs permission.
As if it asked for what
it will remember.

In Rio, in January, the sun
hammers all day at the lampposts.
Children rap all night
on the windows, asking for money.
They will not go away.
Nothing will ever go away.
Not the night with its cheap perfume,
not the arsenic glare on the rooftops.

White flower, white flower, yellow —
they push up through the ground
uncalled for. Planted
by someone else, another eye
determining their order.
I accept them the way I accept
what is not offered.

Touch me, you said, and I did.

The gardenia lasts twenty-five years and still
it is Easter morning.
And there's one white carnation
for the day we were married.
Yellow flowers, carelessly cut
and pasted, tumble from envelopes, wilt
on dashboards. Nameless daffodils, forsythia
spitting back the sun.
Why do I need to make sense of it?

White. White is the color of faith. Of salvation. In Salvador, women spread their white skirts as they sit on the corners, cooking *vatapa* or selling beads. Their heads are wound in gleaming bandanas to stave off the relentless sun. White upon white. And the bleached steps to the churches are crested with women, flowers that rise into the air like flaming birds.

Flames. The beach is a forest of flame. Each candle held in a cup of sand. At midnight, the women walk backwards into the ocean. When they return, dropping onto the sand, dripping and bedraggled, they have left behind their boats of fire. On each boat, a mirror; in each mirror, a candle; and in the water, a million reflections. Fluid, watery light.

Water. We filter it first through a tall terra cotta urn, then boil it for drinking. We wash our vegetables in boiled water. Strange, exotic vegetables, especially *xuxu*, chartreuse, lit globe in the vendor's hands. And rich, red-seeded passion fruit with its musky taste — *maracuja*. The word rolls around the mouth like a marble. Nightsong.

Night. The sound of things on the edge. Jackfruit drops from the trees in the garden next door. Over the tiled roofs, someone calls in a throaty voice. Sometimes a dog. Or traffic on the main boulevard. More often, though, there is an indiscernible hum just underneath the other sounds, something waiting to grow large, something wanting translation.

Want. In the market there are hands inside hands, asking for coins. The man with no legs scoots on his makeshift cart. Children thrust even smaller children into our faces. Their teeth are shattered. They rap on the windows for money. They won't go away. And you — you want too, so you scatter some change and retreat.

Change. Nothing changes. The language circles you like a vulture. Unfamiliar, except in the way you know you will always feel strange in its presence. Noon. The light is so intense that colors spin and give off sparks, like glints of sun on a swimming pool. In the depth of shade, shadows go green and leisurely. They belong to another time, or so it seems.

Time. It climbs the sky and floats there, hazy and unredeemed. Measured in a foreign tongue. Time erupts like a hive, itching the palms, the inner thighs. It flows like a river in January where tropical water has never been stilled to the bone. The sun hesitates, then drops in an instant into the sea, leaving its afterimage.

After. Everything is a dream you might have lived. The words go distant and cold. Flags are furled and dancers spin counter-clockwise on the reel of memory. Once you sang about the quarrel between the clove and the rose. Equatorial songs, bred of abstraction. Now you live in a land of detail. Grass is the softest of greens, and snow is unutterably white.

And then the eye admits it sees too far. The mountains that flattened in the distance are suddenly there, large and purple. Or the red rock, wind-whittled, shifts from left to right. Turn on your own axis. Nothing to fasten on, or return to. The desert keeps its secrets well. Though now, on a day in early April, it seems about to burst. Orange flame at the tip of the ocotillo. And yellow haze of creosote. On the large arms of the saguaro, waiting for evening, white blossoms that will open overnight and attract the doves whose pollen-dusted wings will move again from ancient plant to ancient plant.

No matter how often I might come, this is a landscape I will never know. It resides outside the body, alien and unresolved. Georgia O'Keefe entered the desert willingly, spun in the vortex of its heat. The colors whirled, then clarified.

But my eye hungers for pastures, small hills, lanes. Wants to be cut off from space so vast it reminds me of what is yet undone. Undoing.

Wild poppies in a field of grass: I want that day forever. Skitter of clouds. And a fleeting sense of belonging to the earth beneath me. Not this dun rigidity, resistant even to water. Flash floods cut the road in two. Then this brief blooming — and after, nothing upon nothing, unless the eye is pitched to such obstinate light.

P. V. LeForge

When I was 7, I peeked
through a curtain
and watched my mother
placing ants on her clothes
to crawl up her sleeves
and across her bare, painted feet.
I saw her put them down her blouse
and smile.

We had a thick slatboard fence
around our back yard
so neighbors couldn't watch
as my mother held out her arms
and preened like a sparrow.

As the years passed
I tried to ignore those
moving freckles, to pass them off
as little ink stains
or floating cinders
come to rest.
She never spoke to me about the ants
and I never asked.

For parties, Mother would shower
and dress in sheer decolletage
but I'd still imagine those little tunnelings
under that long silk screen
as they made their winding way
up the back of her neck
and into her beehive,
loaded with winter provisions.
I remember that drugged-sensual smile

with which she served the hors d'oeuvres.
She was always picking lint from her dress,
hitching up her slip, scratching a swollen ankle
with the tip of a high-heeled shoe.
Upstairs when she tucked me in
she would pat that bouffant to sleep
and rejoin her guests.

I'm in another city now.
I don't know if my mother
still dances with the ants,
but lately, I've observed
long lines of black workers
inching up my fingers like travelers
who know their way.
At first I was appalled
and flicked them off my skin
and out of my apartment.
But that touch to my fingertips
was tantalizing.
I wanted more.

It's a vice, I know,
but once a month, sometimes twice,
I drive out to an empty field,
bare my skin to the sun,
and spill little tracks of honey
down my arms and toes.
With a drop on each nipple
and behind my ears,
I let them have their way with me.

SWEATER

P. V. LeForge

While others go to parties
or to the movies,
I stay home and sweat.
When people play hockey or tennis,
I sweat watching them.
I sweat on trains, in restaurants.
I sweat in blizzards.
My bed knows it,
so do my clothes;
but when I tell people this
they shy away.
Other people never seem to sweat.
their clothes remain dry
even on sweltering days,
even in rainstorms,
I put plastic mattress covers on my bed,
but the sweat still seeps through.
Women won't sleep with me.
They're afraid of waking up
floating downstream.
I dream of sweating great torrents
that drown thousands.
It's a habit I can't break,
a cool vice for my hot skin.
My landlady gives me towels for Xmas
and tells me that mine is the only room
in the house not bothered by rats.
Here's my quandary: I want to be liked
but each time I dry my face
or put on a freshly laundered shirt,
my whole body starts to cry.

P. V. LeForge

for Rick Campbell

It's not an ordinary instrument.
Fitted out with a small hammer head,
a beaver's tail staple remover,
nail-pulling jaws,
and a small mouth for straightening wire,
it is the manticore of tools.

At first, I concentrated on the fences,
which are kicked by the horses
and crimped downward by
the spiral grip of honeysuckle vines.
I pounded and pulled and smoothed,
and when the fence was so
straight I could sight along its top,
I learned other tricks.

Searching out and killing
wood ticks, for instance,
was easy with my fence pliers.
I shoed the horses with it.
Then I found that I could use it to
change the oil in my pickup,
fix the bathroom plumbing,
put a new roof on the barn,
pull teeth.

It cures cancer, too.
Draws up the tiny cancer cells
through the skin, picks them clean
and squeezes them flat,
like squashed wood ticks.

But issuing in a new era of life
has its responsibilities,
and I'm afraid of what will happen
if word of this gets out.
Doctors will lose business,
so will pharmacists and casketmakers.
I imagine I'd have a long line
of people at my door and no time
to rescue the fences from the vines.
So I'm not telling anybody.
Just you.

GOLFIN' MATILDA

P. V. LeForge

which, as a title, is not really fair
because this is not about anyone
named Matilda, nor is it about

Jan Stephenson or Karrie Webb or Greg
"The White Shark" Norman and doesn't even
take place in Australia but rather is about

Gabrielle Reece who is over six feet tall
like me and who went to the same Florida
college I did where we both played sports

although I was only on the bowling team
and she was on the volleyball team where
she would smash that white leather sphere

into the faces of her defenders, rearranging
noses and ruining make-up, which was something
she knew a lot about because she

was also a supermodel whose body and face
graced the covers of 93 magazines and 950
websites around the world, including Australia.

The story begins when Gabby turns thirty
and some rich dude offers her a ton of money
if she will take up golf instead of volleyball

so she moves out to a place in the desert
and learns which part of a driver strikes the ball
and that a low score is better than a high one,

which surprised her and it also surprised her
that she could hit a volleyball with her fist
so much straighter and farther than she could

hit a golf ball at first, but Gabby is not only much
better looking than most people but also much
stronger and soon she was hitting 300 yard drives

every couple of hundred tries, which is something
only two other women in the world can do,
neither of which is Jan Stephenson or Karrie Webb

although the White Shark can do it sometimes
and so can I if the wind is right and when
I'm on the tee I think about her out in the desert

slicing or hooking and working valiantly to break 90,
which she has already done although she has only
been playing for eighteen months, and I think

about how she was taught to hit standing on one leg
then the other, to hit it while hopping or with a
crossed grip or with her eyes closed and how she

still loves golf more than modeling or volleyball or
being married and maybe so do I although if I
were married to Gabby I might feel differently.

And if you are looking for a point, it is that
golf has a tendency to consume like a cigarette
paper even if you are a Lady Clairol Cover Girl

or an aging poet and that, although she does not
know me (even though I may once have sold
her a book in my bookstore), although we

live in different states now and have houses that
cost different amounts of money, for four hours
a week, maybe more, Gabrielle Reece and I are true

soulmates just as we are soulmates with Karrie Webb
and Jan Stephenson and Greg Norman and that if
we ever teed up together we would have the time

of our lives just as we do every time we tee up
with our closest friends and I like to think of Gabby
as a strong, flaxen-haired Matilda who would

bring me a cup of water from a billabong or water cooler
on a hundred-degree day, because a poem's title
can't just sit up there and look nice. It has to do work.

THE DIRT EATERS

P. V. LeForge

At first it was potatoes.
We'd buy them at the street market
where they were cheaper
And brush off the specks of earth
that clung to their brown skins,
much like our mother would
wipe the dirt from our sundarkened faces
each evening before our bath.

One night I came into the kitchen
and found my mother licking
the dirt from a potato skin,
her tongue reaching out like
a curious lizard, then retreating
with its discovery back into her smile.
I tiptoed out, but in the morning
the skins were clean.

Soon, I was doing it, too,
and the first touch of earth to my lips
was like tasting the world itself,
smooth and dirty like pudding,
coffee grounds, tar, and pencil lead.
I taught my sisters this art
and soon we had gone from the potato market
to a hillside near our property
where we dug out dry clay with
spoons and sifted it into piles
and into plastic bags
to crumble onto our tongues
when the craving came upon us.

After a rainstorm, we would dig
out the moist clay and bake it
in the kitchen alongside our dinner.
It was our aperitif, our dessert,
our afterdinner smoke. We took earth
like others took snuff and sometimes
our neighbors would join us at the hillside
as we scoured the bank for dark treasures.

On vacations, we ate chalk
or crunchy little chips of starch
until others with the same guilty habit
told us about their own best places to dig.
They told us that English dirt,
the color of soft charcoal, was best
found beneath great fences of stone
and that in Ghana they shaped the
dirt into geometric shapes
and sold them in street markets like potatoes.

It no longer seems strange, this attempt
to take these bits of earth into our bodies
before our bodies are given into the earth.
I like to think that we are tasting
the dust of our ancestors in these little clods;
and that our ancestors, like us, wandered out
to these very mounds, digging with bare hands,
rusty nails, or the ribs of small animals,
for these tiny tidbits, mouths puckering
and glands flowing for their little secret.

CHICA DEL CAMPO

Mia Leonin

I sleep with my heart wrapped around oranges,
One rib unplanted in the field of knives.

Cathedral of old women. Do they know
They are sewing me a gown of beads with their prayers?

Shade of women, working through the heat
Weaving me wings from banana leaves and thistle.

Even bruised, my hips steer these canvas work clothes.
Even untouched, my breasts call the stones to drink.

Only the machetes have noticed my new walk.
They flash their smiles at me. They are cutting me a path to the city.

If I do not leave soon, this town will make a woman of me:
A new tool, a brick oven.

I have an eye on my neighbor's feisty palomino.
I've been coveting my mother's only coat.

Soon, I will tie up my hair and ride towards Cartagena or Bogotá
I will scoop up this God-faced village and blow it into dust.

THE ARTIST'S MOTHER

Mia Leonin

Maybe I did bruise my children.
Maybe I crushed their cries
With the bulb of my cigarette.

Maybe I let them lie
In their own pee
And when they cried to go out

Like dogs, I let them whine
And hunch into corners.
Maybe I turned my back.

Maybe my love ran out
By the thirteenth month
Or in the ninth year

I lay down between chores
And never got up.
Maybe the ticking

Of game show clocks
Tempted me more than their
Garage performances.

Maybe love or decency or even God's will
Can't keep us from the moments
That become entire lives pinched

Into one second, burned
Into one place on the body.
Memories are like accordions:

I have seen them open up
All pleated
Between the hands of my children.

Nothing has made my babies
Sing harder, screw faster,
Paint in bolder pinks and reds.

Even if they don't remember
The house on salt pond
Or the bridgework of shame,

They will always be children:
Curly-headed miners
Counting the jewels between their toes.

Never knowing what
If anything
Really happened,

They lower each other
Below the surface.

MOJO

Mia Leonin

(my grandmother's recipe)

Something from God
A live animal
And something from him.

I settled for a prayer card
The nail of a stray hound
A bite from the supper he'd left untouched.

Grandmother said,
Don't ever ask a mojo to do God's work,
But I did.

You better believe I did.

Mia Leonin

There was a woman who ate the core of every fruit.
Tendril. Root. Vine.
Her insides thicken with the things she has eaten.

Mahogany globe of the avocado,
Wrinkled stone of the peach.
Invisible, fibrous center of the pineapple.

She eats the core the seed the pit the center.
She does not stop at the delicate ribbing of the mandarin.
Not even the luminous center of the coco can fill her.
She begins to swallow great mouthfuls of seawater.

She stops and smells the bark of trees, their branches and fingers.
She lingers and presses her back into tree trunks
In hopes of some fusion, some exchange of calcium and wisdom.

She picks up leaves and holds them in her mouth.
They are extinguished, they are quenched.
She tastes desire in the scent of every living thing:
A twig wants to be a flag,
A stalk of cane groans and longs to be a machete.

There was a woman who ate the core of everything.
She climbs, shimmies, leaps, dances, slithers, and lies down.
        An expert animal.
She stumbles, trips and falters. A mediocre human.

She plucks the tree from its fruit and swallows,
Returning the dark intonation of each stem
To its original amputation.

And beneath the fruit, a palm,
A hand waiting on the other side of her appetite.
To swallow, to ingest. In this way she sets out to know him.

She follows him.
Like a tree follows its own nests and carpenters.
Like a hill winding after its inhabitants.

She follows him like she has followed her own hand some nights
Some afternoons between fabrics and pollutants, between starched cottons
And blue liquids. Liquid medicines. Her hands

She rests her cheek next to his ankle.
She places her neck beneath his wrists.

Like a carpenter follows his wood — jerky gestures, a bent elbow,
she follows him.

Yes, I accept, she declares to no one, to anyone.

She climbs, shimmies, leaps, dances, slithers and lies down.
She stumbles, trips and falters.

Hooved and throated, she gallops with his name flying behind her.
She quakes under his feet. She prays. She dances.
She compounds her prayers with the sucking gesture.
She holds the fruit in the palm of her hand.

And he eats.
Into fractions and decimals.
Into psalms and leftover sandwiches, twigs and damp soil.
He eats. He follows. He runs along side her.
He loses count.

She mates. She names him
She folds her fingers.
She names him by touching his most original feature:

His star-colored mole
His dark-shaped lily

She mates. She doubles her venus.
She eats.
She glistens and skips. She triples her grief.

She commands things. That they transform themselves:
That milk and honey flow from thistle.
That flying animals invert their wings.
She commands that various bodies lift the weight of their own joy.

They lie down. They cannot rise.

She swallows a flame.
He invents the candle.

She turns over and over in her sleep.
He invents the wheel.

She gives off a light.
The crowning begins.

What will we call it he asks.
How will we join it to our hips, she answers.

Nothing so abrupt as singing, the wind lifts their wrists
Leaves rustle and rise up orange. She holds the fire in his throat
And he eats.

HOW THE BRAIDING BEGAN

Mia Leonin

Dear Sister, at three I am leaving.

Where is Miguel? Will I know him when I see him?

Dear Sister, I am leaving with a man who refuses to call me by name.

Bárbara, Caridad, Lázara.

He gave me the names of slaves to choose from.

That first night — his leather sandals.
Three slaves, three saints.
That first night — Miguel undressing from the bottom up.

I chose *Lázara*, of course. Rags stuffed into my mouth.

Here, *déjame verte*. He pushed me against a display window of sunglasses.
Let me see you.

Miguel is not one or one thousand or multiples of eight.
He is many.
So many rooms to ride through.
So many arms to consider.

Siéntate.

Sister, he is from a town called 100 fires where everything is written
in green. Green sleeves, green armbands and pant legs, a green eye written
into every corner. A woman sat on the northeast corner of the plaza sharing
her vocation. Without a watch, clock, radio, stars or sundial she could tell
you the hour. People would pass five and six times a day. Children would
try to trick her. Her right eye was grown over with a cataract, blue and
foaming like boiled milk.

Siéntate. What I thought were wise sayings turned out to be
simple commands.

Siéntate. No stand up. Here let's move into the light
so I can see you better.

Sister, a dress appears.
I am always wearing the dress and then the night and then the man —

Mock slapping my face.

I have wanted this — to be incapable in the language of my lover —
To be so far from fluency — just one new word.

Sigue

One day Miguel happened to be standing behind the woman.
And he noticed that a clock fell right in her line of vision.

Sigue Sigue

He continued to go to her and ask the time.
He watched the children try to trick her and sometimes he did too.

A dress appears.

What I thought were simple commands.

So much green — in his sleeves. In his walking away.
So many possibilities in his shaved chest — In his oranges and rind
and hungry palm.

Mock slapping my face.

One day Miguel realized the hands of the clock had never moved.

Sigue

That first night, Miguel undressing from the bottom up.
Waves biting me, breaking into me,
so many words and their fingers rolling in and rushing out.

I have wanted this —
To be praised excessively in a language I don't understand.
To crawl under a word and listen.

Sigue

In English, the translation would be, "keep going" but what we really
say is "Don't stop" — at the center of pleasure — it's possible negation.
The impulse to cover ones mouth during — the impulse to shield an
exclamation.

Please, don't stop.

Miguel. Now that my fever has lifted take me to town.
He never made it here.

Weave fruits into my hair.
What arrived were his leather sandals

Miguel. Carry me in a basket no matter how big I grow.
Orange rind rubbed into the skin

Sell my hair to the farmers for water.
His shaved chest and hungry palms.

Miguel, when I wander off, yell for me
Like you yell after your child or your dog too close to the curb.

His eyes are still buried in a blue boat
His curiosity lies napping in the one-eyed woman's lap.
His disbelief is burrowed behind her milky cataract.

How will I know him? Where will I find him?

In this story, there will be no other form of aquatic transport
but my braid.

Dear Sister, at three, I am leaving.

I will cast my braid toward 100 fires and it will fan out like a net,
Like a mermaid's tail.

Whoever does not help me is my enemy
Dear Sister, I must find the man
Who gave me the names of slaves to choose from.
Those who do not help me are my enemies.

I will drown the fishermen who tangle my net.
I will wrap them in my dress of shells and seaweed
And dive down deep.
I will drown children and dissidents alike. I will drown

Julia B. Levine

there was no rain,
the air heavy
with unwept clouds,
the sky mostly fallen
over the walnut orchard,
and all that marked a row
inside those stubbled fields,
dissolving into fog.
      Each dusk,
I stood at my office window,
staring at the dull horizon
bruised and fading.
I ran my hands through the sandtray
where children lost
what they wanted to find. Sometimes
my fingers suprised a buried stone
or a tiny angel,
and rubbing it clean,
I tried to return the figure to the story,
the one where he told me
there was no one else,
or later, how a man stood on our porch
holding out my husband's letters to his wife.
      Always there was that moment
turning off the light,
a glimpse of two chairs facing each other,
emptied and flashing back to shadow,
the sound of my shoes on gravel,
the way the road heaved and blurred
until I had to pull onto the shoulder
and turn the radio loud to weep.
      I cried in every room
of our house, kneeling on the pantry floor,
face down beside the sofa,
my forehead cold

against the plumbing of a sink.
I walked after dark
looking for a light in his rented room,
but most times,
even that was gone.
　　　　Hard to say, then,
exactly how misery rinsed me clean,
why one morning
the drowning white of our bed
woke me, linen and calm,
and stepping onto the balcony
I was given back
one minute at a time
to the sun in March,
the first plum blossoms
beginning to unfold.
　　　　Joy was a splinter
I felt as it entered,
while warmth slanted between the rails,
and a hummingbird pulsed
close enough to drink.
I sat with my hand to myself,
the weak sun on my thighs,
a rich briefness of scent,
　　　　almost animal,
how I knew to help the wound
that way, over and over,
palm to touch, to heal.

SALMON RUN
ON THE CONSUMNES RIVER

Julia B. Levine

Muscled black, their yearning
confuses the river's mouth.
One begins a volley of frantic jumps
up the ladder, and hundreds follow,
a slap as each salmon falls.
And here on shore,
a crowd of people press hard
against the chain-link fence.
A woman turns sideways
to make room for us, grey hair
barely contained in a barrette.
She smiles, then brushes a hand
against my youngest child's cheek,
against this wild longing
to draw close and closer still.
It is late in a November afternoon,
every face stung pink with cold,
same color of the sweater
my grandmother crumbled into my arms,
the last time I saw her, blind,
asking my name over and over,
her sad question like a snag
against whatever current pulls us on.
Downstream, black fins cut the water in looping eights.
We climb over quartz and granite,
and from where we sit, finally,
I can see torrents rushing through the weir,
and salmon struggling inside every swell,
the way that woman's tenderness
knocked me, for a moment, somewhere
between the two worlds we live within.

Above us, cormorants perch the wires,
while upstream, fishermen stand knee-deep in water,
lines cast out. In the failing light,
a salmon leaps through the river's slate,
edges broken gold, a brilliant ravine
drawn out, just barely,
before darkness churns back in.

WHEN I NO LONGER WANTED TO DIE,

Julia B. Levine

and was not working back to my father
as he hurled a shuffle of volumes
down the table, madly cracking spines
of Britannica and Asia, so that I had to stare
too hard into the lilac
festering with wasps outside our window;

or even further back to my great-grandfather
nimbly cinching a slipknot for his throat,
cornhusks soaked in vodka and the Jersey cow
butted up against her stall, my grandfather
dragging the hated limpness of his father
away from the barn as it surrendered to fire;

I did not understand that I was returning
to the first time my mother lowered
the new weight of my sister
into my lap and I held on
to all that could be; to the night
I willed my body through the cold lake

into moon, that water bony with light;
or even after my father slammed
out the screen door, how I quietly taped
across the ripped muzzle of a brown bear,
restoring the bookjacket of a river
throttled with salmon. I only knew

that something wanted to keep on
falling through the late summer dusk,
down the Sierras, granite and fir
suddenly opening into barley fields
spindled with dust, floodways gathering
live oaks into the drying loam;

that days apart from you
had brought me down the mountains
to where the longing to be gone
had become this impatience to arrive,
all the wind through my windows
whispering *This is where we live.*

BLACK WHEEL

Julia B. Levine

This is the silence that held me long before you arrived.

This is the bay, hammered a dusky and pewter blue
and across that shore, this is the last of the sun,

before the dark begins gathering
the dead hills in August, the six windows of this sky,
and in each one, a gull, crying out to sea.

This is the deck where we sat cross legged in the shade
of that Monterey pine, looking down at rough wood,

and when our youngest came outside,
to spend herself equally on each of us,
arms flung around our necks, lips full on our mouths,

this is where we both turned away,
heads in our own hands.

God, what it would feel like to drive a nail
clean through that wood and out the other side.

This is the lounge chair you laid across, and slept,
all night, the fog stepping wet and cold all around you.

This is the silence that goes on as betrayal,
as the strange white light in morning,

one harrow starting from the deepest water,
sliding out across the surface, in fog,

and behind it, a black wheel
tamping out that pale bite of flame
as it reaches shore,

reaches the blacktail deer
mostly hidden in the huckleberries, ripe and royal

along the trail, a wild sweetness
just passing over, barely touching

before leaving — no reason, really,
to have ever come at all.

THE VANISHING POINT

Julia B. Levine

Because all things have one,
I go back to that evening in late July,

our children hidden in their fort,
wind billowing through the tenuous rooms

of dusk. I'd walked back in
to find a bat trapped inside the kitchen,

rippled shadows of those wings
passing like rain across my shelves,

the blind and urgent fingers
touching up against a lamp,

our blue glass bottles,
a forgotten, unlatched window.

In the infinite portioning of the hour
there is no shelter.

Step deeply inside any moment
and still you end up here —

a tiny, shuddered heart
knocking helplessly around the cathedral

of revelation and desire,
erasure as a blossom

unfolding through the truth
of all you love,

the only life you ever wanted
chiming

with what slips through.

Julia B. Levine

And this time when she asks,
The world will end won't it?
a black river of crows will be rowing out
above you, heavy oilcloth of wings
working over slanted roofs,
dark tents of sycamore.
She will tilt her small head skyward.
So that watching her, you could almost glimpse
the secret greed of time itself,
while her question hovers, unanswered
in the slight wind of the stars' procession.
Is she remembering that evening driving home?
How she sat beside you, singing
and just ahead, the cars suddenly
slowed, miles of red taillights gathering
behind the frail wall of five people
standing in the fast lane of the freeway,
trying to protect something
you couldn't yet see.
And then you did.
Inside the half-circle of their bodies, a motorcycle
flung against the guardrail, someone
kneeling in the thickening dusk.
Someone draped in a blue bedspread.
Because you felt it then, the past
so full of silence and waiting.
Mercy as it comes
suddenly, or not at all.
Did she take your hand?
You had to keep on driving. Slowly.

THE COUNTRY OF ENUMERABILITY

Robert J. Levy

for R. W. J.

How we can say "this, and this, and then this"
amazes time and again. The objects
dart their minnow glance at us, swimming up
into the glitter bait within our eyes,

until they're trapped and made more beautiful
inside the mind. So it goes in this place —
whether pedestrian, exotical
or derby-dark, the world's variety

of color, shape and noise is made by us
and fed to bursting with our love. Nothing
cerulean is alien to us,
nothing so dun or drab it can't be fashioned

in the makeshift framework of a phrase
or cordoned off in song. We don't create
the world but its diversity. Our act
of naming is a pure enchantment

and the flattering of everything
into a place it can call "home." Sometimes
it happens unannounced. The sun flames red
toward evening, scars the clouds with mystery ...

meanwhile the jaded eye rejects the show
and gives itself to driftwood, clapboard huts
and sand, to be finally collected,
mingled by the brash young finger-painter

hidden deep within our souls. Steamy
evenings, when absence is the visible
alternative to light, the world goes blank

Robert J. Levy

A lisp of grass, a slur of wind …
soft language from the blackened verge
of wood. I am noun gathering
at dusk. It is dying autumn,
cold season of the nominal
when drowsy words go foraging
for winter homes. With no field guide
but instinctive music, one must
move cautiously over such space
as names allow at night, learning
their migrations by listening
to the wind the mind makes searching
in the dark. A net of meanings
is the only tool required
in pursuit, for they are neither
arch nor devious but simple
ingenues of clear intention
in the modifying forest.
Tonight, they light on every thought
with equanimity. Their joy
consists of falling into snares
of connotation, gradually
becoming tangled in the wet
revivifying grace of words.
once captured, they must be possessed
and loved completely, as only
self-created things can be.
The sweet and sanctifying greed
of our delight will chasten them.
imprisoned in our cages
they will shine on us forever,
shine more brightly for being ours.

THE TACKLE BOX

Robert J. Levy

A three-tiered candy case of barbed
mutations, it wintered in the cupboard
till those summer mornings
we plied the Ramapo
for pickerel. Gun-metal blue,
rimed with orange rust from when Dad
threw it overboard, it doubled
as my hope chest those long, hot days
spent angling for his affections.
As guardian of bait, it was
up to me to choose the lures —
spinners, plugs and jigs. Mornings
we always started out with "spoons" —
flat, teardrop shards of polished steel
that hugged the bottom muck for bass
or weeds. It happened early on:
Enraged by the fishes' tight-lipped
refusal to bite, he grew mute
and edgy with failure. I then
began the ritual exchange,
first offering a Jitterbug —
a plough-mouthed, stylized cockroach
he trolled for a while until
it snagged a lilypad. To calm
him down I tried the rubber-skirted
Hula Popper, propeller-nosed
sardines, electric silverfish
that sent out ultrasonic radar blips.
Technology failed. Next he tried
live bait: bloodsucker worms, turgid
purple muscles he desperately
impaled on hooks. The trout
just stole them for hors d'oeuvres.

By late afternoon he said
I'd scared off all the fish,
then he punched me in the arm
and made me row to shore. Climbing into
the car, he swore never to take
me anywhere again. Silent
in the back seat, I was
something thrown back in the stream —
too small but no less hooked for that.
I held the tackle box, imagining
all those sharp delicacies,

ON THE PYTHAGOREAN THEOREM

Robert J. Levy

*If we listen to those who wish to recount ancient history, we may
find some of them referring this theorem to Pythagoras and saying
that he sacrificed a brace of oxen in honor of his discovery.*
— from Proclus

Just as a bell curve is a kind
of breast with meaning, or graphed
hyperbolae can represent
the coy geometry of lust
(the soft curves of infinite approach
and loss), so too I can believe
that when Pythagoras deduced
the theorem, his sacrifice of
oxen to the gods was not
prompted by piety alone.

Was it for the sake of gods
the dumb beasts were spitted, charred and sent
ethereal, to bovine heaven?
Did he believe the theorem had descended,
courtesy of some mathematical
Prometheus, from on high?

I would like, instead, to think
that the electric "click" of certainty,
flooding his mind like light into a room
where only dark had been before,
was like the voice of a lovely woman
reclaiming him into the world.

At once abstract and visceral,
the "ah ha!" of sudden knowing
was like the "ahhh ..." of sexual release
and knowledge struck the belly of his mind
with the neat certainty of wine.

224 ～ from *Whistle Maker*

I would like to think he understood
that truth was not otherworldly,
that a fact may reek of burning meat
and its proper offering must be
the smoke from flesh on fire, the smell
of food and sex, the aroma
(corrupt, delicious) of knowledge —
the smoldering thigh pieces of the beast.

Rick Lott

Teaching my nephew to clean fish,
I kneel on the back porch in dim light,
as though praying to the stringer of sunfish
which flop on spread newspaper.
I show him how to drive the knifepoint
into the brain, pinning the fish
until it stops thrashing,
how to scrape the scales, spattering
over the porch like little stars.

Overhead, moths flurry
around a bare bulb
as I work a bluegill from the stringer
and lay it before him. He sticks
the fish's head, jerks
away his hands when it writhes,
and I have to kill it for him.
While he struggles with one, I clean ten.
The last, an old female fat and purple
as an overripe plum, orange belly
swagging with roe, falls to him,
but he shoves it away.
I push it back to him,
and he hacks at the fish,
finally tugs at the entrails with the blade,
balks at the yellow roll of eggs.
I take the fish and scoop out
guts and roe with two fingers.

After cleaning up, we turn off
the porchlight and sit on the steps in the dark.
Cicadas whine and honeysuckle fumes like incense.
Overhead, an orange moon nests
in the sky, and constellations wheel.
I point out Cassiopeia, Lady of Corn,
and the Great Bear whose blood will tinge
the foliage crimson in autumn,
and Orion, the destroyer,
all speeding away from each other
into the darkness.

THE END OF THE VACATION

Rick Lott

At dawn I left a tangled bed,
Crossed delicate dunes anchored by sea oats,
Drawn by light
Thin and blue as mother's milk,
And I remembered that even the eyeless earthworms
I dug for bait as a boy can tell
Whether they travel toward light or dark.
Scrub pines seethed in the wind,
And gulls quarreled
As I followed the debris at strand line:
Starfish, seaweed, and broken shells.
The ground swell of a distant storm
Shot spume onto the sand,
Gnawing the eroding beach.
I searched the flotsam
For anything lost: coins, ambergris,
A lavender glass globe from a Japanese net.
I found a melting jellyfish,
Composed mostly of water so salty
That to drink much would kill,
Yet seawater and blood are chemically alike.
The pulse of a jellyfish's bell
Is the beating of a heart that must not stop,
For to cease swimming is to surrender
To gravity drawing it toward black depths.
The eastern sky caught fire
As I rounded the corner
To the bay side of the fraying island.

DIGGING FOR SHARK TEETH

Rick Lott

Down on elbows,
Face inches from the chalk bank,
The retired schoolteacher scratches decayed
Calcium, fossil shells pricking his knees.

Shark teeth abound in this dry ocean floor.
On his den wall, they bloom on red velvet
Like the spreading ripples of raindrops.

Since his wife left, he often hunts teeth.
He has confined time —
That swallowed his son in rice paddy water —
To a chart and learned its aliases:
Paleozoic, Silurian, Pleistocene.

Sometimes he dreams of land sunk
Under fathoms of dark water,
Thrashes for the surface moving away,
Wakes sweating, chest heaving like gills.

Successful, he wobbles to his feet,
Swabs sweat from his scarlet face,
Grasps three fossilized shark teeth.

He drinks from a bottle in his pickup,
And gazes down the highway at the pool
Of heat, shimmering black as a tar pit.

RUBY AND THE HUMMINGBIRD

Rick Lott

The ticket-taker stared at the boy
but let him enter a tent
the color of overcooked tobacco,
where a naked blonde
squatted at the edge of a plywood stage
and shot eggs like squeezed melon seeds
into the crowd of laughing men.
Awestruck, he watched her smoke a cigar
in a way he never could have imagined.
A mahogany woman with maroon nipples
lay on a cot with her knees spread
around a microphone
and hummed "Oh Susanna."
He shuffled out through odors of sweat
and starched cotton, and wandered
a midway sensuous as a rain forest,
the colored lights and balloons
like a riot of jungle birds,
the calliope echoing the weird music
of an ancient civilization.

At breakfast, he picked at his eggs
and stared at the plain face of his sister
and his mother's bunned hair shining
like old barn wood in the morning light.

THE BAMBOO CAGE

Rick Lott

By fluorescent latrine lights, I inspected
myself for seepage, fearing the thunderous pain
even more than rumors of North Koreans.
Anxiety was not enough
to keep me out of the village.

I loved the girls' parakeet chatter,
the way their small-breasted bodies lolled above me
black hair hanging, as a willow droops over water
Their faces called to mind
the pumpkin moons of autumn back home,
lovers in dark cars parked in rutted lanes
among the fields of stubble,

When I tried to piss and was gutted by fire,
swaying like a flame over the urinal,
I felt no anger for the girl whose silken friction
ignited the blaze. Our needs were too great,
I was burned clean.

BLUE RAIN IN THE NEW WORLD

Rick Lott

Crossing the Intracoastal on his way to work, he notices
       for the first time
in a while the racks of stored boats, like cells
       in a hive,
and the yellow forklift crawling among them.
The boats dream in their stalls, hulls gleaming
       like desire,
lines coiled, compass roses as still as seeds furled
       in darkness.
He knows this feeling, for he has huddled on the beach
       at night,
constellations firing his skin with cold light,
       his body
a knot of flesh aching to become open space.

At midmorning, a blue-black immensity of cloud collapses
       into rain.
Shutting down the rock crusher, he takes refuge behind
       steamed windows.
If this old Ford were a boat, he'd sail it to a new life,
       an island
open to the ocean at every compass point.
But he gets only as far as Hambone's and parks among
       Harleys and pickups.
Bourbon makes the rainy morning a luxury, light
       glimmering from bottles and pyramided glasses.
Bearded construction workers stride through layered smoke,
       bikers cluster
like buzzards over the pool table in the back, and an old
       drunk on the next stool
listens to the dark behind the mirror.
A pit bull, its scarred head bulging with muscle and
       teeth, lunges
against the camper shell of the truck parked outside the door,
       snarling

at a startled pedestrian, striking the Plexiglas window
      that bars the blurred world.
Drinking hard now, the crusher explains to the bartender
      how he loves the weather
that drives boaters from the sea and golfers out of paradise.
But a long-haired Indian, his face a dark moon, looms
      in the mirror
and asks, "Barkeep, can you turn that up?" The jukebox bass
      throbs,
and the Indian and a woman in toreador pants sway
      in a circle.
It all comes down, he thinks, to a lone Seminole hiding
      in the swamp
of a waitress from Ohio, the way these workers shelter here
      in the darkening winds,
the looming hurricane a great saw blade shredding palms,
      storm surge
unsettling the present, sailboats hurled into streets, houses
      sucked out to sea.
The storm's ruin will leave a world as fresh as a green
      shadow on the horizon,
and a gust of anticipation sweeps through his veins
      like the morning bourbon
that makes the light mellow and rare, for who has not
      secretly desired apocalypse?
Its seeds lurk in the chambers of the revolver jutting
      under a biker's shirt,
in the teardrop tank cradling a high-octane charge.

Rick Lott

1

My. Am. Me.
Say it like that and you'll know why so many
      come here.
Along the beaches, condominiums rise white as polished
      limestone,
and the spires of yachts jumble against
      a lapis lazuli sky.
Pelicans squat on pilings and never blink.
The North suffers its pall of snow, and people
      pale like memories.
Here, even in the yards of the poor, oranges glint gold
      in jade leafage,
and the sea never gives up its longing, surf nuzzling
      the ankles
and thighs of swimmers, who wade against the undertow,
      or let
waves wash them ashore like flotsam.
Yes, this is the Technicolor life we sought,
      oiled bodies
soaking in salted light, beach umbrellas luffing,
      blue water
strewn with dazzle like crushed glass on asphalt.

2

Each morning and afternoon, the pyramid soars beside
      the cemetery.
Burnished orange or gold, depending on the angled light,
      it takes fire
as rush-hour traffic scuttles by. And what secret lies within,
      what bundle
of dust and leather rules this vain dominion? The man
      driving home from work wonders,

What rich asshole is buried there? Or is it merely a
      mortuary's gimmick?
And a can of beer sweats in his hand powdered gray from
      labor in the pit,
feeding limerock boulders into the maw of a crusher
      that shudders and roars.
And crushed stone is trucked away to fill swampland, the
      fecund stink and ooze,
and rains like brimstone on the creatures scuttling
      in the muck.
Home at last, the man, wearing his dusty face like a mask
      of silence,
sits on the stoop and imagines how tomorrow's sun will ignite
      the gilded tombs,
and the apartment-hive at his back trembles.

3

On an inlet bridge, a boy holds a fishing rod
      and stares
at two women dancing on the bow of an approaching yacht,
      both barefoot and drunk.
The kohl-eyed blonde pulls her bronze breasts free
      of her spangled party dress
and cups them for the boy; the dark woman smiles up
      and waves like a beauty queen.
Hola, America! he gasps, as they are swept out of sight
      under the shuddering concrete bridge.

Erika Meitner

The way we sleep to-
gether is locational,
seasonal — the way

you can buy useful things off
the roadside here in
summer passing through: peaches,

heirloom tomatoes,
squash, sweet corn, bait, antiques, rugs,
tie-dye, fireworks, guns —

your hand around the back of
my neck in the dark
above the covers the way

you'd hold a beer can,
near empty, out on the porch
before tossing it.

ELEGY

Erika Meitner

(for M.)
You shall not make any cuttings in your flesh for the dead,
nor print any marks upon you.
            — *Leviticus 19:28*

When you left
        I stopped everything, or was it

that everything stopped? The mail
        piled up unopened. I knew blind

what the envelopes held
        under their dumb flaps: birthday

cards with wishes, bills
        with owed amounts; no grief

manual. I sat on a cardboard box, tore
        my clothes, covered the mirrors with sheets,

even read the bible, got nearly all
        the way through Leviticus — sin and sacrifice,

offerings and making yourself holy, until I couldn't stand
        the unmitigated commands — *You shall*

and *I am the Lord your God.* Remember us at eighteen
        driving barefoot to Weir's Beach for tattoos

singing, *Freedom's just another word*
        for nothing left to lose? I picked

the exact spot on your back for Tom
        to stencil some goddess sign you'd found

in a book and flinched watching him work his black-ink needle
        into your flawless skin the same way I would

years later when I caught sight of the sunflower-sized bruise
        on the top of your thigh. *Drunk and fell down*

the stairs you said, waving me away. You stayed
        for a week and went back to him. I didn't have the courage

to command: *You will stay. You will*
        leave him. And every night you're with me now,

running from his apartment, robe streaming behind you
        in darkness, him following, him beating

your head against that glass
        phone booth, the neighbor's car.

After sitting low
        for seven days, you whispered, *Let me*

go. I took a walk

around the block, let you pass
        through the front door with me, kept

walking to the local tattoo parlor, had your name
        dragged across my chest so I could

let go, the way we scrawl down lists so we're free
        to forget exactly what it is we want

to remember. I was at the Museum
        of Natural History today —

dinosaur bones set carefully, dioramas
    of Neanderthals in cases reenacting hunts, and an exhibit

on body art entitled "Marks
    of Identity." This is what I learned:

that in the afterlife, where all things are reversed,
    dark tattoos shine brightly

to illuminate a path
    for the dead. I learned

that women shamans
    painted their bodies

with vicious snakes and jaguars
    to protect them in journeys

to the spirit world. I learned
    that the female body

must be marked
    before it can serve

as a vehicle
    for the spirit.

THEY ARE ALWAYS DOING INVENTORY AT THE ALL-NIGHT DRUGSTORE

Erika Meitner

I like driving
to the all-night drugstore past midnight,
sometimes with the windows closed,
air-conditioning on, singing
to embarrassing music, sometimes
with the windows open, letting the dark
roll in.
        They are always doing inventory
at the all-night drugstore.
                I forget that I'm lonely.
People move slower at night.
Not the guy rushing in for condoms on the fly
because he got lucky
        or the uncomfortable sick
tortured with sudden congestion,
with vicious stomach flu, searching
for Sudafed or Pepto-Bismol.

I'm talking about chocolate and shampoo,
glazed aisles easy with fluorescence,
q-tips, crazy glue. We glide in flip-flops
and frayed shorts, in yesterday's underwear,
in wrinkled restaurant shirts, names patched
across the pockets, for blue nail polish, cotton balls,
Bic pens, tissues, lint rollers, Windex;
for the red-smocked employee
stickering gauze with a vengeance, rocking
back and forth on her knees in First Aid;
for the beeping metronome of price gun;
        for the red-eyed man
reading antacid bottles; for *The Enquirer,* near the register.

In old movies ether vapor
caused unconsciousness when inhaled, made patients
glamorously helpless and insensitive to pain
            the way TV's stay on
all night in humming houses, radios play
in every midnight car.
            Hugo, my cashier, is measured,
thorough, shockingly polite at check-out, asks,
Have you found everything
            you were looking for?

My car propels me farther
into the summer dark, cut with the illusory blink
of fireflies, stoplights, signs
that never go out.

Erika Meitner

In bed you grabbed a handful
of my hair, said *it's beautiful,*
reminds me of the black girls
I used to date in high school.
It was raining that night,
120 percent humidity,
and while I answered sarcastically,
I'm glad I could provide you
with a moment of ethnic nostalgia,
who wouldn't want a little of sixteen back?
The octane of palpable heartbeat
when "in-like" was a state
as real as New York, when just nearness
to the opposite sex was epileptic,
in darkened rec-rooms and
childhood bedrooms, parks
and parked cars. For me,
it's Drakkar Noir, cologne of choice
boys bathed in before house parties,
left trailing in visible waves
down beige tile hallways.
I still have a magazine sample
of Calvin Klein's Eternity
sandwiched in an old journal —
I peel it open and suddenly
I'm scrawling permanent bathroom graffiti,
driving barefoot in the summer, fitting in
to skintight jeans again and humming
like a strummed guitar to New Order's
"Bizarre Love Triangle."
If my hair — the mess that broke
school photographers' combs,
the untamable mane that held
number 2 test pencils in its curls
and got me in more slut trouble

than my mother's imagination
could conjure, even with her devout
leftover 70's Semitic afro —
if my hair brings you back
to wherever *there* is, trembling
in the graceful brown arms of some girl,
sixteen, cocky and fragile,
and scented like an entire family
of Jersey Mafioso, then praise
the magnificent Jewfro, the unruly Hebro.
I've spent hours ironing out the kinks,
but maybe it's time to roll au natural
and thank its tangled ways to youth,
the body's new knotted desire, its slow
unraveling at the root in corkscrew tongues.
Amen.

Erika Meitner

men to her house
she straddles the roof
they alternate turns
coaxing her down
they wait in the street
which spins on its axis
the wind gets monotonous
with purring fumes
exhausted trails
of hooked alarms
bordello rungs extended
everything is red red red
and waiting

take this light (night-swim)
take this sound (wing-span)

traversing the acrobat sky
she is jet-propulsion
and shy with crowned stature
divines the *go* relay's
fast-bursting signs
a car starter coughing
the hymned power-lines
bellies of dogwood leaves
wielding their fur she is
armor-ready   hyper-aware
poised on the edge
like a zipper's pull

if the moon is a portal

a gate to the real
like panties like heaven
a palace of skin
her fall will unlock it
a finger running
her lover's spine
a key a bolt tearing
one gold tooth one
gold star at a time
from the sky's body
eternal partner in crime
the strings that hold her
all want no pain only
breathless brilliance bring

PREFACE TO AN OMNIBUS REVIEW

Judson Mitcham

Do not write poems about poetry. Commit
no epigraphs, object poems, homages to anyone.
Please, no more elegies for your father. No details
of your grandmother's hands. Leave the sepia
photographs alone.
        Give us no
Guggenheim-and-here-I-am, bored-or-overwhelmed
poetry. Don't write about divorce — no ironic
meditations at the playground or the game.
Nothing on the limits of the language.
        Construct
no ugly poems ragged on the page, but nothing square.
Go easy on the birds and the trees. No asleep-
in-the-deer-stand, waking-to-an-eight-point-buck-
only-thirty-yards-away kind of poetry.
        And no
remember-that-cafe-in-San Diego poems
of heartbreak; not one Rilke imitation;
nothing modeled on the Spanish; nothing spoken
as Osip Mandelstam or Akhmatova.
        If ever,
on a clear summer night,
there's a baseball diamond in a small town, a field
lighted like a scene in a glass paperweight,
an old man loud in the stands — don't even think it.

If there's something you believe in, have the decency
to keep it to yourself — no revelations, no irate
manifestos on the Earth or deconstructions of the bed,
no upper case god. There should be no nuns,
no old Baptist hymns in your poetry.

           Employ
everything you need to make it happen,
that momentary stay against confusion, but include
no catalogs, no dogs.

Judson Mitcham

Our father always said, "Remember this:
however good you are, someone's better." Every March,
teased by an early warm day,
my brother and I, both backyard stars,
resumed our climb toward the majors.
Maybe Greenville for a while or Chattanooga.
Who had not spent time with a farm team? Still,
we expected Ebbets Field.

And our father's sad logic didn't hold. All it took
was the sports page pulled from *The Journal* —
Willie Mays in the league's top spot, or someone else.
But the spot itself was there, so why not us?

I think of all the days when he came home late,
the light nearly gone, walked straight to the yard
in his tie and good shoes, threw us batting practice,
hit us hard ground balls; and repeatedly,
because we were afraid, showed us how
to play the ball and not to let the ball play you;
to take it in the chest if you had to.

I can see him there, balanced on his toes,
in a low crouch, ready for the grounder —
how the tie that he had thrown across his shoulder
has slipped off now, falling nearly to the dirt,
his eyes still fixed on the ball coming fast,
as if that one chance were his last.

SURRENDER

Judson Mitcham

We were ordinary men,
unable to embrace each other fully —
to bury a face in the other man's neck,
to rock like drunks in the doorway, saying
goodbye. It was always a handshake
and maybe that sideways hug,
with an arm around the shoulders.
            In the hospital
you couldn't understand, didn't know me,
tried to overturn the rack by the bed, tear
the needles from your arm; searched everywhere,
underneath the sheets and the pillow,
for your clothes, *going home;* grew frightened
when confused by the purpose of a spoon, angry
when you couldn't even urinate — failing
to hit the plastic bottle, till I held you.
If I leaned down close
when the baffled agitation started up,
and I smoothed back your hair, or I kissed you
on the forehead or the cheek, whispered "Daddy,"
you'd throw your arms around me.

There's a way a man turns to a woman,
so his lips just barely graze hers, yet in this,
there is everything that follows, each detail
of forgetting where they are.
And today I am trembling with desire, wild
for the years, when my lips feel yours, cool
as gold. One kiss for the infinite
particulars of love, to tell you this:

I will be with you there, in the darkness.

AN INTRODUCTION

Judson Mitcham

You who break the dark all night, whisper and shout,
who travel in and out of all the rooms,
who come with pill or needle, vial or chart,
with bedding, mop and bucket, tray of food;
who turn, clean, pull, read, record, pat, and go;
who see her hair matted by the pillow, greasy white
wild short hair that will shock
anyone from home who hasn't seen her for a while —
shocking like her bones, showing now;
like the plum-colored bruises on her arms; like her face
when she first comes to and what it says; like her mouth
and the anything it says: *Call the dogs,* or
I've got to go to school, or *Tonight y'all roll
that wagon wheel all the way to Mexico;* you
who have seen three children — unbelieving, unresigned —
in all these rooms, full of anger and of prayer;
you who change her diaper, empty pans
of green and gold bile she has puked up; you
who cannot help breathing her decay,

I would like to introduce you to our mother,
who was beautiful, her eyes like nightshade,
her wavy brown hair with a trace of gold; Myrtle,
whose alto flowed through the smooth
baritone our father used to sing;
our mother, who would make us cut a switch,
but who rocked us and who held us and who kissed us;
Myrtle, wizard typist, sharp with figures,
masterful with roses and with roast beef;
who worked for the New Deal Seed Loan Program,
for the school, local paper, county agent, and the church;
who cared long years for her own failing mother
(whom she worries for now; you may have heard her);
who was tender to a fault, maybe gullible,

as the truly good and trusting often are; and even so,
who could move beyond fools, though foolishness itself
delighted her — a double-take, words turned around,
a silly dance — and when our mother laughed
(I tell you this because you haven't heard it),
the world could change, as though the sun could shine
inside our very bones.
      And where it's written in Isaiah
that the brier won't rise, but the myrtle tree,
there's a promise unfulfilled:
she will not go out with joy.
Still, if you had known her, you yourselves,
like Isaiah's hills, would sing. You'd understand
why it says that *all the trees*
of the field shall clap their hands.

PHILOSOPHY, WITH ILLUSTRATIONS

Judson Mitcham

The paperback history of thought
cost fifteen cents. I discovered it
in a box of old books at a junk store, where
it now belonged, ruined by a child

with crayons, who had reddened Heraclitus, and who,
as if choosing to ignore or revere
every word set down in between,
had brightened up Schopenhauer, bearing down hard

with an orange and a green. Standing there
waiting on the book's once blank last page
is a figure with its arms set to fly;
with a body like a one-lane road;

with fingers like the petals of a sunflower, head
ballooned, hair floating just above
like a cloudy idea or a cloud;
with hollow round eyes drawn large; with perhaps

a smile, though it's easily a grimace,
on its one thick deep blue lip.

NOTES FOR A PRAYER IN JUNE

Judson Mitcham

1

The other boys lived,
and a prayer grew from this:
the unbelievable sadness of chance
and the shattering dazzle of glass still strewn,
days later, on the road.

2

My son won't let things go, and I love
his fighting to understand, in his own terms.
Having learned about light years, he recalled
the distance to the school, how heavy
his legs felt when he raced there.
                                    What form
will his knowledge of the wreck take,
when he learns how, late one Sunday,
twenty Junes ago now, I flung you from the world,
through a windshield?
                        Will I tell him
how I ran to get help,
yet tired, had to slow down, my legs turned to lead,
had to rest in the face of death, how far
I have traveled through the years?

3

I remember the late spring night we camped out
on Alcovy Mountain, just the three of us
who later on would take that ride.
We laughed at ourselves for playing war.
We were nearly sixteen.

And it seems like a last act of childhood,
crawling up the north slope
so softly I could reach for a branch,
draw a bead down its gnarled barrel

and laugh you dead.
                              The next morning
when absolute darkness had failed, for a while,
we stood without words above the world,
a white mist drifting far beneath us
forever, over homes we were headed for.

                    4
Is it breath rising in the Christmas air
as a child pedals up and down the driveway at dawn?
Is it dizziness with which
a woman has to reach for the words
to send into silence with her son?
                              Each June,
it's the brief taste of salt, licked away,
as a boy hurries out to the street, having breezed
through the hot kitchen, kissed his mother's face.

                    5
Before our eyes, that heavy old coin disappears,
while it stays where it is. We're aware
sundown is a lie now,
though we see it the same. Chimpanzees
pause, sometimes, from their foraging or play,
sit quietly and gaze into the west
until moved by darkness.
                         Perhaps, in their eyes,
nothing seems magical, or it all does. From us
comes a forced, final nod toward the sleight
of relentless method, how it turns
pure mystery to laughter in the end.
                              Still,
we know there's a magic we begin with, tricked
by love's act into this ruled world.
                    — for Glenn Hawkins, Jr.

THE TOUCH

Judson Mitcham

— for my mother

You stepped out the back door, drying your hands
on a plain white apron
and watching me slap the new basketball down
on the driveway's nearly flat hardpan,
unable to control it or to stall,
for long, its falling still.

You held out clean, wrinkled hands for the ball,
let it drop and caught the rise
with the fingertips, never with the palm,
allowing no sound but the ball's hollow bounce,
crouching low, either small hand
moving with the ball.
                    And years later,
when the Newton County Rams came down,
like the cavalry at dawn on a few Cheyenne,
in a hot-breath man-to-man press, the best plan
was to get the ball to me. Even now,
I return to that late fall morning
when you taught me what a softer touch could do,

how to go where I needed to, never looking down.

PERSEUS APPEARS
TO THE THREE GRAY WOMEN

Jean Monahan

What a different world it might have been
were it not for the man

who stepped out of the wind
shaped the way our dreams had always shaped him.

What hues might have blazed, if not for his fire-
colored cloak and bronze shield, charcoal hair

and copper skin? We remember now his smile
curling up, smoke-thin, from the lid of a scowl,

how he watched us watch him, all the while
gauging our hands, as we passed our one eye

beneath our gray wings. The exact moment we lost
sight of him remains uncertain; under the pregnant

clouds that impound our land there is only this
sudden, heartsick wonder: in a careless

moment one might blindly trade
the world into a stranger's hand.

PIANISSIMO

Jean Monahan

The day my brother lost his finger
(he and his friend laughed it up out back,
slipped the blade of the shears through the hedges,
the digit no bigger than a twig
finally found) I sat down
at the piano and played my lesson
through twice, perfectly, without making
a sound.

THE BONES OF POTTER'S FIELD

Jean Monahan

We have fired so long in this great wide
kiln the clay is bleached with our calcium
our skulls reshaped into cups and handles
our knees cracked bowls our hips halved jugs.
When they bear down with their shovels to dig
another in, the rich sand turning over
the way leaves turn over in the wind, whole
dark slices rain with knuckles. In the field
to bury strangers in out of our newly
gleaming bones we assemble the One who
will rise again.

A LETTER TO ROBIN SILVERMAN

Jean Monahan

*On July 30, 1985, a pair of Siberian tigers attacked and killed their
zookeeper Robin Silverman as she cleaned their cage at the Bronx Zoo's
Wild Asia exhibit. A volunteer who accompanied her (and for whom it was
the first day on the job) escaped by scaling the 11 ft. fence. Zoo officials
stated that Silverman, considered very competent, had violated the 'cardinal
rule of animal care' by entering the cage without knowing where the tigers
were. Her accidental death was the first in 86 years at the zoo.*
      — New York Times, July 30

*Correction: Officials said today that Silverman's chores had not included
cleaning the tiger cage that day.*
      — New York Times, July 31

Though such a death is not easily
conceived as chosen, I often imagine you
standing there: skillful fingers hesitant
for an instant on the gate's lock; the flatly

insistent morning-light awash on your face;
how, in its pale, high relief, your assistant
must have seen minute hairs, fine as new fur, prickling
across your cheeks. Had she known, what else

might she have seen; rigid intent in a sidelong glance,
a warning flush as you let yourself in? Trust
is reckless, a human trait; at the last moment
she saw, with ferocious clarity, your terrible mistake,

bristling at the alien pleasure of close-range.
Beneath the greenblack cover of imported brush, two pairs
of eyes opened like glittery flowers as nostrils
quivered awake; tails wagged in lazy crescents.

Wild Asia was spurred to instinct.
However I choose to understand what brought
you to the fence, I bring my own hand
up to the latch. There are no cardinal rules

in the treatment of one human by another. In the teeming air
of our narrow escapes, we freely observe our species
advance, capable and composed, toward
extinction, increasingly eager
for what must appear,
as it approaches, more beautiful
and superior
with every step.

QUITTING COFFEE

Jean Monahan

Bruised, hoarse, I crawl out
of the woods after years of feeding on roots
and the long bones of wild animals.

Already, my ability to see at night
is fading. The soles of my feet
soften like soaked burlap.

I lived in a tree, I slept in snow.
Down on all fours, I could leap
straight up and take a deer.

Now, eating with a spoon,
I watch the mouths of those
who feed me. I can no longer feel

the moon, stroking my back
with bony fingers, the jittery
whisk of fire through cattails.

The mouths make such sounds
as wind in winter. I listen hard, harder.
So I return to the fold: wild-eyed, still craving.

LESSONS OF THE EYE TEETH

Jean Monahan

Every smile hides a bite,
the fear of being left out;

in the cheek of every scowl
is a wad of hope.

The need for caution is real:

the saber-toothed tiger could be killed by a kiss,
the history of the world is engraved in the tusks of elephants.

If only the mouth could see itself,
could taste the danger in every hunger.

Nothing tastes as good as it looks,
but the eye teeth, just learning to see,
can't discern this.

Inside the blind, soft cave
of the mouth, Wisdom arrives
in a burst of pain, and too late.

WOMAN FALLS ASLEEP DOING THE SUNDAY CROSSWORD

Jean Monahan

Too tired to rout the words
hidden behind the clues, you
paused on the stair joining
ogham and *owl*, and bowed
before the puzzle's paper tyranny,
an uncapped pen brandished

in your fist. Good soldier,
it stood guard all through
your dreams, trailing your
thoughts along one arm,
then dashed between ear,
eye and mouth, bleeding

itself dry with so many
messages. By daybreak,
you were your own
manuscript. Whatever stumps
us — leaves us at a loss for
words — folds over our sleep

like a flimsy tent, a matrix
of nouns, adjectives and verbs
we labor to connect. Last
night, your oracle sat, as
usual, at the intersection
where three routes meet.

Imagine her delight at
the pen in your hand,
a slim sword to cut the cord
between your two minds,
the one that sees, hears,
and says, and the one that

denies, denies, denies.
Learn to trust her inklings,
her scrawl, her stab
in the dark when all
else fails. Learn to read
what the blind hand writes.

THE KISS

Jean Monahan

We've been saying something like this
For months: slow-ripened sounds
Wafting out of our mouths the way
The hot sweet sweat of cut hay
Whispers and lifts out of a noon field;
Setting each other in our sights
The way the black and white and staring eye
Of the egret fishes: with precision,
Interpreting the light, the ridged waves,
The streaked and mottled back of the catch;
Leaning nearer, close enough to watch
The beloved vein in the neck fire, see
Salt on the lip, the whole forest smoking
As the meteorite burns a swath.
I tell you now, the glacier may take years
To advance, but it never stops moving.
The eyes of the wolf are bigger
And hungrier than we remember.
Look at how my mouth yearns toward yours.
Far at sea, a small swell aims for shore.

ABOVE DALTON

Michael Mott

where we were standing when the rain walked round us
with a jingle of mule tackle on the piney air
and a cat snicker of hog flesh twisting on a stick
like a live snake trying to get itself up
backing out of the fire
and a jug of buttermilk

brought by some girl so lean and piney herself
in her wet shreds of floursacks my heart hit me
not for love but the poor peakish look of her
and for bringing up buttermilk

coming up that mountain in the snarl of a spring morning
to a camp of men who were no better than you'd guess us
and setting the jug down on a stone like we'd ordered it
and going off without a smile or a word down the path she'd come up

above Dalton one day in the war when the rain walked round us

SOURWOOD MOUNTAIN SONG

Michael Mott

like a saw snagged in wood
ten years and every word she said
the whine and the clasp of grain

a line of Byron and an old song
about Miss Mousie and the courting frog
and the war came and I was roving
and the teeth stopped in the log

then the silence was like a knot
even when bullets snapped trees
I was listening always listening
and the killing went on over my head
like the tune of a liquored up fiddler
and the boards bucked under the dancers' feet

and I went roving in the moon
the woodsman's moon and the soldier's
and ached for the listening and thought
of the bullfrog courting and Miss Mousie
and the small white teeth of the saw

and nothing of this I shook off
till I came to Sourwood Mountain in the Spring
and hung up my gun and drank cold creek water
and saw the leaf claws on a rock like a bear's
and the gold sand in the bottom of the stream

and made up a song to go with the circle
I'd walked any weather and under the moon
how the fiddler'd be sawing there still
and how sourwood made the sweetest honey

CHIMBORAZO

Michael Mott

Chimborazo Hospital, Richmond, 1862

On Chimborazo, Richmond's canvassed plain, say that I walk
more than the wards — whose feet make no peaks in the bed —
move through the sulfurous air and clouds of floating lint,
to stalk a bandaged sky, swing upon starry lamps, or spread
great sheets, cool caterpillar tents, over those lying far
beneath me on the larval floor, poor fluttering wingless
things, scorched there by their own eyes, automatas who wave
bound limbs to pluck the sting out of the blowflies' whine.

Say that I walk before them like an insect god. Christ walks
on Galilee. The locust walks the wind. The mantis, holly twigs.
The whirligig walks water. I climb rungs of fire, or rise up
with a wheel, whose fans blow on their remnants, rally living
back, until they turn cold gold below me, crack their yellow
mask, and smile — as if bird-priests had touched their veins
with magic blades of jasper, freed the lacquered earth, the
armored heart, spun jaguar calendars back to mists of origin.

De Leon's lure lost in gray cypress swamps and live oaks
wound with mummy cloth, black mud, and orange water. Say that
even here, like some white egret, heron, insect-bird, I rise
into the higher air. I circle, circle slowly, float, the ghost
of every shadow's hope, each burning atom's opposite in ice,
pain's poppy dust, hell's heaven, thirst's water, drowning's
land, youth's age and age's youth, whatever's not … my limbs
on Malvern Hill, my gangrene dream sleep walking and awake.

LABOR DAY WEEKEND, NORTH GEORGIA

Michael Mott

Thunder, the cardinal flower out by the creek
so rich a red in the cricket loud
cricket green weeds under a pewter sky.

Ticking from slashed mattresses and fawn
chicken feathers wander the yard
where roots wear through the stamped clay.

All the resources of emptiness are reached
in the corners of outbuildings. A calendar
from a funeral home is eight years out-of-date.

The nail it hangs by bleeds a long russet line
dividing Christ from the door he knocks on
in Jerusalem. Everything draws in

a perceptible second. Violence of rain.

MEADOW GRASS

Michael Mott

for Marie Mellinger

There is more to this meadow under the mountains than mere names
of fescue, blue Timothy, panic grass, foxsedge, hopsedge — but my eyes
keep coming back to the dark strokes of plantain, each head as if surrounded
by a ring of pale insects, a curious, almost ugly crown

The Cherokee called these weeds "Footprints of Englishmen" —
wherever the settlers went the plantain grew, broad leaves
escaping under their heels, the wayward wagon tracks
grew like dark stars on the banks of a Devon lane
seen here against clay of the same colors: oxblood to orange
foxbrush, fernseed, the outrageous rust of men
washed into creeks in the runoff of heavy rains
mingling Greek blood and Trojan
like Scamander in the old tale
some settlers had by heart, and more never heard of

The roots of red flowers went to the chiefs and warriors
Yellow and white were squaw flowers, went to the mending of women
Children sucked on the creeping stems of the pea plant and grew eloquent
in a language that no longer mattered. It was the settlers' names
that caught up with the changing meadows — wort, balm, and bane
Gerard and Culpeper claimed them

Not the Seven Bark, nor the lovecharm Pipsissewa profitted
in the eclipse of the Sun Spirit and the Star Maiden
only the transplanted plantain — spear, vinegar sponge, corona of insects —
only the Deptford Pink, Venus's Looking Glass, Mouse Ear …
The weed-strong invaders clung like pea plant to the alien clay

I would escape a moral if I knew how
or remake one if I could stop my wandering
The grass changes under my feet. Words, names, change in my mouth
under a shifting, mostly indifferent sky

AUGUST, ALCESTE

Michael Mott

"Time will soften this, the dead count for nothing at all ..."

Low tide, late afternoon when Santa Marias
with wind tight, sunlit canvas fill the pools.
The window curtains signaled as you came in sight,
uncertain freight of thought, you thought you saw her.

The sunless house you ran to was the same and yet it wasn't.
You noticed for the first time in the bedroom
how in your wedding photograph her veil
billowed and streamed across the shadow.

      Alceste was here
who left no fingerprints, no footprint;
Eurydice who at the outrage of a cry
gropes her way back through ear shaped caves;

Grace Kelly, Marilyn, Diana ...
Persephone holds all in thrall. No earthly spring
will spring the locks, empty these wards of winter.
This afternoon borrows no second beauty.

Her veil, the years' white wake, a winter's tale,
stops at the frame. The songbirds sing
over the moving marshgrass. Sweet voices.
Alceste, say nothing final till I mend my song.

PIANO AT MIDNIGHT

Michael Mott

You stop your walk along the beach.
Someone is playing Scarlatti.

The night is dark about the lighted window.
The vast sea settles quietly.

Someone alone is playing for everyone awake.
All debts are canceled. All are free.

NOT-SO-SECRET LIVES:
HOMAGE TO TISSOT

Michael Mott

Talented to the point of no return, a certain slickness,
not mediocre, very bourgeois, Monsieur Tissot, coming to grief
first by a revolution, then a love affair in England;
twice wrecked, not nice any longer for the nice to know,
those quite predictable as patrons, schooled in erotica
by Etty, Alma-Tadema, and Ingres; those educated in the orgies
at some removes in print, read in all innocence
in the *Times* law reports, among the pilloried for
unnatural vice, overindulgent lust, or impropriety, Monsieur Tissot.

No, not the first or greatest artist "skyed." Storm in a teacup.
The order of release for Mrs. Newton, twenty-eight, and very lovely,
if we believe James-Jacques-Joseph, and who can doubt it,
who sees her do the Grecian bend and gaze behind her
under the autumn leaves, gold hands of the horse chestnut?
          Very lovely.
And fragile, too, to ride a storm of scandal for him.

Elsewhere — exquisite nose, eyes sad but bright, Irish complexion —
she climbs a none-too-steady stairway, feeling her way
up to the captain's deck under the flags and bunting.
You sense the subterfuge, the coded names, the haunting
of hotel rooms warm with the glow of gas fires.
How much that light flatters her skin. How very brittle
the gaiety put on to please the foreign painter.

The Doe at Bay. Better perhaps than drawing-room boredom,
to flaunt her flags, for once admit her beauty.
Refinement needs a risk to be refinement, she's aristocratic
under her furbelows, the Anglo-Irish, very-English, Mrs. Newton.
Her sensuality is veiled, but not at all uncertain.
It was a secret she but hinted at, yet he reveals it.

To paint his love was one thing. To exhibit her, another.
Only a refugee could feel the need perhaps,
his art apart, to test a new indulgence.
Valor of ignorance ... This was no Odalisque, no dead hetaera ...
This was another's wife, so clearly Mrs. Newton.

Virtue, one cynic claimed, is often envy.
Good Englishmen forgathered to destroy him.
Good mumbling Englishmen, a canting crowd,
insured their hidden selves. But who can blame them?
Plainly she was not Helen, he was indiscreet, and this is London.
Storm in a teacup. Quite. One soiled Victorian beauty —
though "soiled"? (here Envy speaks) — and one unstable foreigner.
"Goddesses," yes, they might have called their wives. But real goddesses
don't pose in autumn parks hiding a wedding ring! I wonder.

Pathos, not tragedy. He was not Raphael, nor even Renoir. She
was Mrs. Newton. Then what power translates them
a little beyond storms, his talent and her beauty?

Ann Neelon

Today I am braver than Mamadou Bamba.
I'm ready to juggle cabbages and teach everyone my real name.
Then I'll go woo all the vegetable ladies for carrots and mint
and flatter the fishmongers into giving me *tiof.*
I feel so strong today I may even throw stones
at the *bana-bana* men.

Look, today the market brats are thumping out my entrance
        on upside-down tomato cans.
They know I'm fierce enough for warpaint and tam-tams.
Oh bless them, the little thieves have stopped picking my
        pockets!

The little girls have all forgotten how to hiss.
How generous they are, roasting peanuts for their mothers
and picking flies from babies' eyes.
The cashews they sell taste like apples.
I am so courageous today
I may let them plant cornrows in my hair and pierce my ears.

What, have I grown a beard today or memorized
the Koran in my sleep?
The old men keep biting into hard bread
and recommending me gustily to Allah.
Today they expect me to answer important questions
about the nature of the universe and the circumferences of
        circles.
I drink strong coffee and put my feet up on rotting banana
        crates.
I spit tobacco,
then chew on a weed to clean my teeth.
How peaceful it is
sleeping under these black umbrellas!

Those cunning mounds of flesh, the lettuce ladies, are already
smacking their lips but I am too quick for them.
No more squished tomatoes!
Today I insist on fresh okra and live shrimp.

And for heaven's sake, no more rotten eggs!
I am so angry about the past that I tumble
all their eggshell pyramids and make puddles
of dead chickens.
Now they're afraid to make fun of my husband.
I tell them he kills elephants and keeps me happy all day long.

Oh, the marvelous cuts of meat I will buy today:
ribs dripping with blood, glistening sausages,
bone marrow fit for teething lions.
No more oxen fed on sawdust.
I have been hunting so long today I am really hungry.

And who are all these second wives clustering around the onion men?
Away, away, bickering women!
Can't you see Machmou and Abdoulaye
are taking you in with a grain of salt today?
I can read the palm of every bay leaf.
Do you think they'll make *me* pay for garlic?

PALE MOON OVER KIGALI

Ann Neelon

Like everyone else, I've been riveted to Rwanda,
to the dead bodies of Tutsis floating downriver as if toward me —
black bodies bleaching strangely white in the relentless sun.

Here, it's April, dogwood season, paroxysms of blossoms in our
        front yard.
I'm pregnant for the first time ever.
Whenever I look in the mirror, I see veins flowing like swollen
        rivers to my breasts.
I am just beginning to feel a body moving inside my body.
The movement is fluttery like a breeze.

"Chaos: A Vector Analysis" is a friend's reading
of the ultrasound pictures I hang on the refrigerator.
I'll admit there's something inchoate about them, but I can
        recognize
a shadowy body, even if I need the white arrows
to identify the parts: head, nose, chin; hand, wrist, arm; heel,
        foot, toes.

My belly rises slowly like the pale moon over Kigali.
In May, I hear a telephone interview with an American missionary
        who survived the massacres.
She says, my neighbors were poor — they didn't use guns, they used

        machetes.
Outside her compound, she sees the hacked-up bodies.

I am terrified of birth.
I am terrified of death.
In the bathroom one morning, I convince myself I have had a
        miscarriage.
I am embarrassed when I discover that the blood clots are the red
        peppers I had for dinner.
By July, the Hutu refugees have begun pouring into Goma.

I watch them dying like flies from cholera and being wrapped in
        straw mats by the roadside.
An old man crawls on top of the dead bodies
French soldiers are already bulldozing into mass graves.
He refuses to move.
He believes it is foolish to waste the effort.

"Do you think the Tutsis will kill you?"
A clubby reporter interviews
a hollow-eyed Hutu boy
who has lost his mother, father, and six brothers and sisters
on the road to Goma. "Did you ever *know* a Tutsi?"
The boy answers out of a deep cave:
"My mother. My mother was a Tutsi."

In the seventh month, I begin to lumber, like a cow in a thicket.
When I get up to go to the bathroom in the middle of the night,
I hear sorrowful mooing I'm afraid is my own.

My husband is worried
about the diagnosis of gestational diabetes.
He sighs when he puts his arms around my big belly,
as if he's convinced it will do no good
to measure the circumference of the troubled world.

Every Monday, we hear our baby's heartbeat.
We're not afraid to confess how much hearing it awes us.
It's as if we hear drops of the most incredible, most viscous
        sweetness
dripping, dripping, dripping from a secret faucet we ourselves have
        turned on at the center of the universe.
There's nothing demure about this sweetness,
which rolls in like thunder when the nurse turns on the fetal
        monitor.

On the late news, I hear that refugees flooding out of Rwanda are
        being trampled to death.
All night, my baby keeps me awake with its strong kicking.

Ann Neelon

We are humbled by the vehemence of the earth,
which must finally have taken our sins to heart.
In this emergency, we begin to understand seismology, life and
      death colliding like tectonic plates.
Apocalypse is a radio broadcast: *I am standing outside a building*
      in which human beings are burning alive.
Last weekend, in the mountains, quaking aspens were a
      prefiguration.
It is still October, but we no longer whisper *beloved autumn flame.*

Nor are telephones immortal creatures.
In the first of thousands of aftershocks, we tremble into their ears:
"Mother, father, sister, brother — I was true to my habits. I am
      therefore alive.
I was not driving on the freeway when it collapsed — a foolishness
      of which you accused me because today is no different from any other
in only *one* respect: you insist on loving me to absurdity."

In the blackout, it is back to Genesis. Television undreamed of,
World Series eclipsed by earthquake, sacrifice upon the face of
      the deep.
"Let there be light, let there be light," cries out an old man
twenty years too fragile for the crowds at the ballpark, too
      senile to remember
that baseball was not invented until the seventh day
when God rested because the din of life, not death, gave Him a
      headache.

Somehow, in a nightmare's dictionary, baseball becomes a synonym
      for faith, hope and charity.
Perhaps the catcher in his death mask strikes awe in us. Simple-
      minded in the aftermath,
perhaps we all grope toward the same analogy: the earth is to a

baseball as the hand of God
is to *my* hand. Or perhaps, when the earth opened up to swallow
     us,
we wore a baseball diamond on one finger like a jewel from the
     bowels of the earth to help us pray:
Compel us, like black coal, to scintillation, in this twenty-second eon.

The dead begin to appear to us as baseball stars in pearl grey
     uniforms.
The moon is a shadowy baseball we ask them to autograph.
The host on the radio talk show is unequivocal — *the World Series must
     be cancelled* —
but we do not defer to him. We rise for the National Anthem.
We sing sweetly, in spite of ourselves, like child prodigies
     shipwrecked on a desert island:
Oh say can you see, oh say can you see the world is not ending, the
     world is beginning again.

Ann Neelon

for Sheila

Our faces were standing pools.
Somehow, your suicide bred in them.
We were afraid of stirring up
trouble, so we didn't ask questions.
It was the early summer of our lives.
The trees were luxuriant in their leaves.
We have almost forgotten.
If only we could say to you now
help us remember.
Help us remember
how green the trees were,
how green we were too.
Help us remember
how one night we took our sleeping bags
up to the top of the hill beside the playing fields.
We were so used to seeing everyone run around
in the bright sun up there
that it was strange seeing everything dark.
Help us remember how we looked out at the city.
It was a small city, but we thought it was big.
Its lights shimmered like diamonds.
Help us remember
how graduation was only a week away.
How we were exhilarated, but also afraid.
How at 5 a.m., the mosquitoes got us,
which was OK because we couldn't sleep anyway.
How we packed into an old car, drove to a diner and ate breakfast.
How somehow we belonged with the loquacious drunks.
Help us remember
how pretty soon it was really morning.
Then again it was evening.
Morning and evening, evening and morning,
first jobs and grad school,

weddings and houses,
husbands and children,
and now it's been 25 years.
Sometimes, on early autumn evenings, we see clouds of mosquitoes.
Your death whirs and whirs.
Its persistence is infuriating.
Our sweetness is something it still wants or needs.
Its sting still surprises us.
We still reach out and swat at nothing.

Ann Neelon

"Believe me, they're no angels," I say to strangers on the sidewalk.
One stands at my right, the other at my left.

But they must be angels.
Otherwise, how could I serve as their handmaid,
today as ever bowing my head,
washing load after load of dirty underwear.
Nothing is impossible with God.

I fear them, swords crossed, on the archivolts of everyday.
Such fury in their eyes!
Mom, he's lying.
He hit me first.
No, he hit me first.

One of them wrestled his way up a ladder at 18 months old.

They both fly out to me
the millisecond I pull into the driveway.
Behold my dinosaur!
Behold my rainbow fish!
Behold the letters A, B, and C!
They swoop down from the sofa,
the coffee table,
the posts at the end of our driveway.

One day, one of them got lost in the supermarket.
For a few minutes, it was like I was without my Guardian Angel.
When I was a little girl, I used to confuse
my Guardian Angel with my shadow.
If there was no shadow, then there must be no sun.
The universe must be dead.

The road is dark and long.
I hope they will tell me, at the end of it,
"Be not afraid."

Now I lay me down to sleep.

They will knock heads over my deathbed.
She's mine.
No, she's mine.

Naomi Shihab Nye

At 7 a.m. a driver from a car service comes to collect me on the drizzly upper east side of Manhattan, where I'm a houseguest. I need to go to Paterson, New Jersey, to stomp around with junior high school students for the day. *Paterson, New Jersey, please,* I say. And the driver with his beautiful accent says, *Tell me, how do you get to New Jersey?* Is he kidding? I live in Texas. I know how to get from San Antonio to San Angelo. Obviously we must cross a bridge or traverse a tunnel to go from Manhattan to Jersey, but which one? Beats me. *Call your office,* I say. He doesn't have a phone in the vehicle.

So I urge him, *Pull over* and find myself trumpeting out the window, *How do we get to New Jersey?* at every third corner. No one looks surprised. Lean Latino men step closer to help us. Sleepy grandmas point damp newspapers. And they know. They all know something. If we don't speak to strangers — what will we do in a moment like this? I translate everybody's fast English into slower English for my driver. He is careful with his pedals. He bobs his head in that graceful subcontinental way. As soon as we're safely tucked onto the George Washington Bridge, I ask where he's from. *Bangladesh.* I've been there. *Twice,* I tell him. He turns his whole head around to look at me. Smiles. Every driver I've had in this city is from Pakistan, Palestine, Trinidad. It's a federation of bravery — the city's wheels steered by the wide world. *You saw my country?* he says brightly. *I saw it. I didn't drive there though. I didn't either,* he says. *I just got my first driver's license. Three months ago when I arrived here.*

We miss an exit. Actually, we miss a whole level of road. He says cheerfully, *Oh my goodness! We wanted to be up, but we are down.* Then he says, *The first time I was driving, someone wants to go to Newark Airport. I don't know it. I say where is it and they get very angry. They are shouting, Drive! Drive! They are telling me where to go. Actually that is what my company says — you only learn by going. When I leave them, I try to come back to New York City, but two hours later it is dark and a policeman by the side of road tells me I am going to Florida. Florida! Did you ever go to Florida? Pull over,* I say.

We roar into a gas station where I ask a lavishly tattooed man about Paterson and he tells me. Luckily there is not much traffic in our direction this morning. We are able to ease in and out of the flow. Now I am growing worried about my driver getting back into Manhattan with the horrendous traffic moving the other way. We pass houses with their eyes still shut, worlds we know not of and worlds we know too well. Kids with book bags. A thousand little turn-offs. Graffiti and pink trees. *Is it nice in Texas?* he asks me. *Very nice,* I say. *You could drive there. A lot.* Finally we pull up in front of a brick building in Paterson where I think I am supposed to be. Fifteen minutes early. *We made it!* He turns around to shake my hand a long time. *My friend!* he says, *We made it, yes we did! And I don't even know how to ride a bicycle!*

MINT SNOWBALL

Naomi Shihab Nye

My great-grandfather on my mother's side ran a drugstore in a small town in central Illinois. He sold pills and rubbing alcohol from behind the big cash register and creamy ice cream from the soda fountain. My mother remembers the counter's long polished sweep, its shining face. She twirled on the stools. Dreamy fans. Wide summer afternoons. Clink of nickels in anybody's hand. He sold milkshakes, cherry cokes, old-fashioned sandwiches. What did an old-fashioned sandwich look like? Dark wooden shelves. Silver spigots on chocolate dispensers.

My great-grandfather had one specialty: a Mint Snowball which he invented. Some people drove all the way in from Decatur just to taste it. First he stirred fresh mint leaves with sugar and secret ingredients in a small pot on the stove for a very long time. He concocted a flamboyant elixir of mint. Its scent clung to his fingers even after he washed his hands. Then he shaved ice into tiny particles and served it mounded in a glass dish. Permeated with mint syrup. Scoops of rich vanilla ice cream to each side. My mother took a bite of minty ice and ice cream mixed together. The Mint Snowball tasted like winter. She closed her eyes to see the Swiss village my great-grandfather's parents came from. Snow frosting the roofs. Glistening, dangling spokes of ice.

Before my great-grandfather died, he sold the recipe for the mint syrup to someone in town for $100. This hurt my grandfather's feelings. My grandfather thought he should have inherited it to carry on the tradition. As far as the family knew, the person who bought the recipe never used it. At least not in public. My mother had watched her grandfather make the syrup so often she thought she could replicate it. But what did he have in those little unmarked bottles? She experimented. Once she came close. She wrote down what she did. Now she has lost the paper.

Perhaps the clue to my entire personality connects to the lost Mint Snowball. I have always felt out-of-step with my environment, disjointed in the modern world. The crisp flush of cities makes me weep. Strip centers, poodle grooming and take-out Thai. I am angry over lost department stores, wistful for something I have never tasted or seen.

Although I know how to do everything one needs to know — change airplanes, find my exit off the interstate, charge gas, send a fax — there is something missing. Perhaps the stoop of my great-grandfather over the pan, the slow patient swish of his spoon. The spin of my mother on the high stool with her whole life in front of her, something fine and fragrant still to happen. When I breathe a handful of mint, even pathetic sprigs from my sunbaked Texas earth, I close my eyes. Little chips of ice on the tongue, their cool slide down. Can we follow the long river of the word "refreshment" back to its spring? Is there another land for me? Can I find any lasting solace in the color green?

THE URGE FOR EPASOTE

Naomi Shihab Nye

Just because she overhears someone say how pinto beans are no good without it, suddenly she has to have some too. Even though she never heard of it before. What it might be to live without such longings she imagines as the sadness before people kill themselves. Visits grocery stores till at last a small packet of dried in the Tex-Mex market where you spin a roulette wheel to find out if you get your groceries free. Makes beans, dumps in whole packet, eats. And not even memorable. Nothing like cilantro was, first time. Later in Mexico, living in a house with an epasote bush flourishing outside the door, starts putting it fresh in everything till she knows, *knows* what that woman meant. Opposite of dull. But you have to teach your tongue. Tongue has to want it on its own. It can't be *mental*. Back home she finds a single small pot of epasote tucked in among basils and lavenders at the nursery, plants it in ground, waters till it grows bigger than a horse stall. Wind galloping through jaggedy leaves. Lets it go to seed. Gives it to people who never heard of it either. To a young chef, with recipes. Stalks as long as arms, *grow into this*. Tied bundles, string. And keeps her ears open. Next thing you know.

THE ENDURANCE OF POTH, TEXAS

Naomi Shihab Nye

It's hard to know how well a town is when you only swing through it
on suspended Sunday evenings maybe twice a year. Deserted streets.
The dusty faces of stores: elderly aunts with clamped mouths. I like to
think Monday morning still buzzes and whirls — rounded black autos
roll in from farms, women measure yard goods, boys haul empty bottles
to the grocery, jingling their coins. Nothing dries up. I want towns like
Poth and Panna Maria and Skidmore to continue forever in the flush,
red-cheeked, in love with all the small comings and goings of cotton
trucks, haylifts, peaches, squash, the cheerleader's sleek ankles, the
young farmer's nicked ear. Because if they don't, what about us in the
cities, those gray silhouettes off on the horizon? We're doomed.

ALL INTERMEDIATE POINTS

Naomi Shihab Nye

If today you are going to Buda, Texas and the bus rolls into Buda, Texas and stops, you climb down and you are ready to climb down. Perhaps you sigh, make a great heave-ho. It has been a long trip. But if today you are going to St. Louis or Pittsburgh and the bus passes through Buda, Texas and someone else climbs down, it does not seem like a long trip at all. This has always fascinated me. And if you are sitting in a bus terminal and the muddled loudspeaker announces ALL ABOARD FOR DEL RIO AND EL PASO AND ALL INTERMEDIATE POINTS, does the phrase "all intermediate points" wash over you pungently as the scent of bus terminal hotcakes and do you eat them one at a time?

CINNAMON TWIST

Naomi Shihab Nye

We did not mean to hurt my mother's feelings when we filled out the application form in her name in response to the HELP WANTED sign in the window of the bakery. She was startled to be called for an interview regarding a job to which she had not applied.

We were trying to ease her loneliness. She & my father had recently moved to a different city, leaving both their children behind. She had not yet found many new friends or activities. My father & I were taking a walk together in the unfamiliar neighborhood, discussing her melancholia, when we saw the sign.

It was not the first mistake in anyone's life.

She could walk to work. Passing the groomed suburban houses in their impeccable isolation & the ragtag apartments & the cleaners & the video store & the grocery where the carts bunched up around the poles in the parking lot by early afternoon ... wearing a hat against the serious Texas sun, perhaps a straw hat she might wear to work in a garden ... carrying a purse with her wallet, a coupon for Handi-Wrap & one for cat food ... what did you do in a bakery besides measure, mix, bake, arrange, slide new trays onto shelves, dust crumbs, talk to ladies wearing nice linen jackets or tank tops, take orders, fill sacks, make change?

It sounded comforting.

Cake doughnuts or French? Glazed or powdered? We did not know about the secret album under the cash register that people would ask for in a glinting manner, or that our own mother would be asked to lift it forth & open it before their eyes, cakes shaped like breasts, single or double, with luscious nipples, the giant pink or chocolate penis cakes, the Sock It To Me! cakes, innuendoes of plump cleavage sculpted into lemony icing. That she would have to ask, this way or that? about things she had never discussed either with her children or husband or her own parents — sparkles, ripples & curves. Where the candles might go, for example, in such an instance. Who the cake should be delivered to, exactly, & what was the occasion, what words should be inscribed?

It is easy to imagine her never smiling through any of these transactions, keeping a stern face, taking the money as you would touch something that had fallen into a toilet. She blamed us. Sure she did. As if we had known. The thought of these things being baked into cake had never occurred to me on this earth, even in my oddest fantasy, nor to my father; the two innocents, as we depicted ourselves during her rages. To us, the only thing to worry about in a bakery was what kind of shortening they used in the cookies or how long the cupcakes had been in the case. We had tricked her into bondage to a bakery of shame. *So quit!* we begged her. *Quit!* But her German Lutheran upbringing which said something about never running from a task once your name was on the time chart was something we could not reckon with.

I think a few seasons passed. People in leopard-printed coats bought cakes for bachelor parties. Secretaries selected long cakes for wild office bashes. A mother bought a cake for her son who was turning 18. My mother glared fiercely, slamming her money down. My father & I lived in fear. Of course large numbers of people who knew nothing about the secret cakes dropped in to pick up regular sacks of cookies on their way home from the drugstore or glossy red cupcakes for a great-nephew on St. Valentine's Day — these were the people my mother lived for, the pure hearts, clean of ulterior intent.

Eventually, she eased back into Montessori teaching, her preferred & regular vocation. But I think she was marked by the album under the counter. It left a shadow in her spirit, a spooky truth — your most familiar people could open the door to the underworld without even knowing it & not be able to rescue you, once you toppled through.

THE WORD PEACE

Naomi Shihab Nye

You could find words or parts of words
inside other words, it had always been a game.
PEACE for example contained the crucial vowels of
EAT and EASY which seemed suggestive
in good ways. If people ATE together
they would be less likely to KILL one another
especially if one were responsible for shopping & cooking
& the other for wiping & cleaning & you took turns.
Then you started thinking, what does he like?
What might suit his fancy?
There should of course be meals
at all peace talks, yes, we understood that
long ago, as there is eating at festivals & weddings —
the generous platter, the giant bowl.
Those who placed a minor faith in rhyme,
might try PEACE & CEASE, as in,
could you please CEASE this hideous
waste of time & resources, when's the last time
any of you considered how lucky we are
to be BORN? We had grown too far
from the source, that's for sure.
A man spit ETHICS at me as if it were
a dirty word.
And what about apologizing to kids, hey?
After TEACHing them to use words to solve
their differences, what did we do?
People two years old were starting to look
a lot better than people than anyone else
& consider their vocabularies.
EAT was probably in there.
Sweet DREAMS & PLEASE which also contained those
crucial vowels found in PEACE if anyone
were still thinking about it. This didn't always work

though, because some might say WAR contained the
first 2 letters of ART & you would not want them
for one minute to believe that.

SORTING METAPHORS

Ricardo Pau-Llosa

We are like water spilled on the ground
that can never be gathered up again.
    — 2 Samuel 14:14

I open the glass and it hovers out
and back from the garden, a few feet,
inches at first, then more ambitious,
and back to knock against the screen,
until the fly is free of the thought
of this screen between us. We may
live a whole life between
two unyielding and unseen boundaries,
until something opens and,
reluctantly, we swing out and then
there is the metaphor of looking
at urban maps, those two lines
are Dominguez Street where I walked
as a child to the Covadonga's
white colonnades and lush
gardens, more a palace than
a hospital to my eyes, my ears
filled with the baroque lamentations
of its fountains. There
white robes recline on terraces,
healing in the Tropic of Cancer.
Only a map is left of that Havana,
major buildings towering
pencil marks on a grid,
half the city fitting under my spread hand
moving back from P-K4, lightly
arched fingers, the opponent's
intense sight and clicking of his time,
then suddenly a gesture and my clock
starts again, Q-Q7, Check,
and again my hand hovers back

from the move, not too certain,
a fatal miscalculation? My arm's
silhouette across the board
as dawn breaks over Quartre Bras
and cumulus shadows move
toward a soldier half-dressed
stepping from a ruined barn,
the weather advancing
from the Sambre River to his darkness.
It is a time of retreat, of tricolors
drowned in summer mud, of possible
misfortune, says the seeress,
when the ace of clubs comes together
with the four and six of clubs
it is almost certain death. Sad,
I know, but not irreversible;
we have our cards to warn us.
The six is separation, the ace
a long, long journey, and the four
is your deathbed, its four posts
you see, or at times the four
legs of your writing table,
which could mean, perhaps but unlikely,
that you are an author and will write
about death and journeys, and so
there is nothing to fear, no cause
for your hands to tremble.

THE RED HOLE

Ricardo Pau-Llosa

A burning rose,
the cupped palm of a martyr,
a flamingo crushed by a truck,
a bite-mark in the throat,
an apple-bloodied eyelid, a copper
penny like a drop of frozen blood,
a Revlon-red cell
whose mitosis is speech,
whose nucleus is a kiss,
a quark, a neutron, a button,
a chalice, a red postmark,
a cut bone, a petal,
a beachball glowing like a lit stove,
a period in red ink on a student's paper,
the heart's comma, a drawer knob,
a rusty keyhole, a drop of acid on skin,
a round flame, the sliced artery of a corpse,
ringworm, the eye of a moth, an open
parachute, the rope-burn of the sky-diver,
a target, a bullet hole in the temple,
an arrow through the wrist, the wax
seal of a letter, a stop-light,
a hole left in a cheek by a laser beam,
the sun setting or rising, a fingerprint
in blood, a digital-clock zero, a nipple,
a fiery magnet, a blood sample through
a microscope, the hole left by a pulled molar,
a fertile ovule sliced in half,
a tear in Caesar's robe,
the horizon moon, March 6th, 11:34 p.m., on the beach.

Ricardo Pau-Llosa

The way a hand startles when waking
suddenly, we see it self-poised
in a knuckled, private will,
sheet marks still fresh from sleep
across the face, arm, and palm,
is not unlike the way, half-buried
in some somniloquence, you walk
full robed onto the costly terrace,
your violet and darker violet
caftan sailing up from you
as you water your *Cattleyas* and *Oncidiums*.
Our condos parallel each other
anonymously, each a notch
in a switchboard of bronze glass
and balconies in order rising
to scrape the baroque,
semitropical atmospheres
with Malthusian mortgages.
You are the lady of the twelfth
floor, bishop-colored with a greying
knob of hair exed by nacred pins,
head anchored by an amber necklace
from Kush. You have followers
that blossom on other terraces,
heads uncombed by Freud or mistresses.
One shares the view from the 19th
with a paste-jeweled poodle.
Another with a golden wrist clicks
into prayer like a pontiff grasshopper.
On the right the roar of a jet
jars this vertical, urban mime,
and we all look up thinking together
that it might blow up and we
would be the only witnesses,

our faces on the evening news
shattered with grief like the jet's
windows, blossoming on TV sets
the way we do on these terraces
in clear sight of which the plane
moves on and away,
its smoke trails blazing into swans
that will never nest on our cool floors.

PARIS INUNDATED

Ricardo Pau-Llosa

for Ron De Maris

The city is a reef
where crabs decorate
cornices, angel fish
pass through windows
like smoke, jellyfish
stab onto TV antennae
like kites,
turtles huddle on the curb
with a windblown homburg,
plankton travel the paths
of indifferent spores,
and minnows shift in cosmetics
departments, watched by an octopus
draped over the head
of a mannequin.

On the bakery shelves
anemones and sponges.
An eel coils
around a billowy dress
worn by a warm upcurrent.
In office corridors
barracudas knife
sealed envelopes, dwell
above leather-bound rubble.
Triumphant arcs halo
schools of sardine, and an obelisk
points to whales catching
their breath, their cumulus
shadows darken the unstrolled gardens.

But it is the shark
who alone possesses the ornate galleries,
the emblemed vaults. His fins
scrape the headless wings of tumbled victories.
He is the new dove bursting through
the rose window of Notre Dame.

OSTIONES Y CANGREJOS MOROS

Ricardo Pau-Llosa

For what seemed to be the whole night
he burned, an effigy on the coast
commemorating the day of St. John. It stood

above a pyramid of trash, itself made of trash,
his jewels falling to the pyre at its feet,
the glow eclipsing night and Havana.

The flames increased the giant and all around
people stood at a safe distance and gazed,
a human halo watching a flame the shape of a man,

a man turning into a constellation. That morning
I had seen on the dog tooth rocks of the coast
a nation of urchins and among them mollusks and crabs

clinging as best they could or dancing upon the charge
of broken tide, the sea rising and falling like breath
in the dreamer's chest aspiring life into a flesh

whose mind was lost. Did the mollusks dream the terror
of the tides around them, and could that dream bring
safety into these shells gripped one to another and to rock?

The dreamer knows he is on fire and that his flames
catch on the wet black concaves of the mollusks and blind
the crabs' tiny orbs, their minute claws snapping

at the misplaced appearance of the sun. With each breath
the flames grow and break into a thousand brief stars
toward the sea. The world burns, it's true,

but he is serene. In the charred morning
he will walk among the tiniest lives that circle him.
Already we lift our eyes and arms to him in welcome.

Ricardo Pau-Llosa

Below, the parceled land,
neatly shuffled farms,
a Nazca
of practical lines.

Traffic, armies
working the white arteries,
hairlining forest
and plantation greens.

Chance would have me
a foreign native
sick of distance,
counting the lofty days

and miles above Cuba.
Through a cobweb of scratches
on glass and plastic,
I see through clouds

and gauzy tears,
wounds of vapor
whose chaos seeming
determinations —

the pull of temperature
on the draft of current,
precisely thrown
by impounded steel —

present maps myriad
as the seconds,
a land in blurs outlined
only to be

engulfed by number
and trajectory,
to be given back
suddenly in a blow

of horizon,
then taken again
in a white theft
into the climate vest.

The vapor fills
the host of window,
and it is then I see
my native country

at last, the soil of minutes
in anchored months,
the howling soil
of the everyday.

Blank and dense,
unbroken,
a white syllable,
prescient as a handmirror

that tells what it must,
as in a rigorous
corridor, of these things
passing, the rotten

lurchings. And here and there,
the beacon principle
breaks out
from the blankness to rhyme

heart and the green
and toil of nativity.
To deceive with belong,
to lose

us in the finding.
I know now
by watch and principle
what lies

beyond my home filled
with simple emptiness
is the palette
of sky and sea

we reduce to blue
for language's sake,
to think it
and go on.

CANTALOUPES

Francis Poole

What do de date matter
what do it matter

How the wind don't blow
the rain she black
and nasty as boogers

The city she a naked stranger
with worms in
her hair
and red teeth

The neighbors they
they might as well be
alive
but they dead
upstairs
and rotten like
old cantaloupes

What do de date matter
What do it matter

The moon now
she all clean and
white as bone ash
She up there grinning
like a crazy woman
making me dizzy

Francis Poole

Enough was too long:
Patient as a handrail,
the past has emptied now
of all who lived here.
The house my grandfather built
sits beneath a late summer sky,
swabbed with the chill iodine
of evening.
Cued by the fading corona
a water-tower collision light
begins to flash and flash,
flagging down the night
around its soybean field domain.
I am vacant with this house
and anxious to be absent again.
The empty room remains itself,
an echo-chamber or translucent
like glass blown hollow
through the nerves.
His three storied relic,
now lodging my vision, vibrates;
as if matter become aware
of itself could speak.
Or would.

CAFÉ AT ST. MARKS

Francis Poole

From nowhere I surfaced
in the bright café
staring at a sailfish
nailed to the deep blue wall
like a superreal sculpture
of a sailfish nailed
to a deep blue sky
until my eyes grew fins
and swam upstream
like blind fish
around the bosom
of a laughing waitress
who smiled through odors
of smoked mullet and
sweet onions frying
and offered me a menu
brushing scales from her
deep blue apron

HIS OWN TWO FEET

Francis Poole

At dusk the streets are nearly empty.
The walls of the buildings glow flamingo.
A young boy walks up the hill pushing
a wheelbarrow filled with the hooves of cattle.
The smell is rich.
He smiles at the tourists who are
sickened at the sight of his burden.
They are headed down to the marketplace
to buy shiny leather jackets, belts and slippers.
As they pass
the boy's own two feet
become hooves, flint-hard and deadly.
He hears them click against the rough stones
of the street, growing sharper
as he pushes on.

— *Tetuan, Morocco*

Francis Poole

And open the window.
Now sit down in that old leather chair
and let's talk pianos.
If a piano had thoughts
what would we make of them
as they go brightly tapping across
the blue marble floors into
the wonder moon room?

The piano was invented by Tuareg goat-herders.
Don't believe me?
Okay, we'll skip that part and go straight
to the first time I heard a piano
in glorious Technicolor.
I must have been six or seven.
I was coming up the stairs
followed by bouquets of purple irises
and pink fuchsia.
It was like being chased by
a gaggle of naked servants
and marionettes. All sweat and clatter.

Some years later I head my grandmother's piano
in the cold, ghostly room called "her study."
A black lacquered upright
that played like a Japanese rake
making yin-yang patterns in the dirt.

And my father once took me
to a piano petting zoo where
white and black geese
pecked furiously at the handfuls
of grain scattered at their feet.

I also worked in a pottery shop
which had a piano. A *Paradiso* I think
or it could have been a *Diablo*.
Anyway, in the afternoon
all the blinds would be lowered
leaving only yellow straws of light on the walls.
Nothing louder than dust falling.
The blond shop girl would rest her
tendril-like fingers on the keys and reveal
Ol' Jelly Roll's Blues in
sinuous, serpentine chords whipping
back and forth like an ox goring melons
in the market, spitting seeds and melon juice
all over the walls.

That was piano as Holy mollusk
curving out of its pink shell
and slapping kisses
up and down my spine,
arpeggios flying like fish scales
scraped from tail to gills.

I was always a little afraid of the piano —
afraid it would slam the keyboard cover
down on my fingers
if it didn't like my style.

I'd bet that right now
a piano sits at the bottom of the ocean
its eighty-eight keys playing notes
as they sink one by one
through gelatinous clouds
of rotten wood
to the silky mud below.

A song once sung by Pharaoh's
seven green-eyed daughters
as his coffin was laid in its tomb.

Francis Poole

Alone on the tracks
between here
and the nearest town.

Overhead
billowing clouds.

Silver rails
hold the red freight
perfectly still.

RISING EARLY
THE LAST DAY OF OCTOBER

Francis Poole

Standing at the kitchen window
I mistake my blue reflection
for a frightened stranger.

My suspicious neighbor
the bat-winged moon
sits perched among the broken ribs
of the trees.

I am here to boil the water,
make the tea, and when
the hooded carpenters arrive next door
absorb the first hammer blows.

Just offstage the sun
tries on different masks:
phoenix, mandrill, blood-red skull.

An owl shrieks.
My empty coffin coated with dew
collects its first ash.

FORGETFUL ANGEL

Keith Ratzlaff

Memory is a minimal condition.
— Kirkegaard

Here I lose
my own hands
even in my own lap

But that's not the point

Here everything
is performance
which is heaven's great secret

Now and now

Here memory is not minimum
but minimal
not little, but least

Like a mask but thinner

Like the moon — whose motion
isn't memory
but the act of being the moon

I've forgotten how to say this

I remember rain
I miss
the way it wandered

through the entire
afternoon
The way the world settled

The cat's red dish
the rain
gradually filling it

Action and not plot

God is a chair
to sit in
and the act of sitting

It makes all the difference

And yet rain, how it was
like something
here and not here

Like a ring once on my finger
Like a road
disappearing in the trees

GROUP PORTRAIT WITH UKULELES

Keith Ratzlaff

Once I was a boy
in a classroom
of boys learning to play

the ukulele. In the end, even
the stumpfingered
learned three chords:

G, C, D7. Our big felt picks,
our whiny
little strings. We were a part

of the American Folksong
Revival
in spite of ourselves,

in spite of our penises
and voices
rising and falling like elevators.

Imagine us, our 25 faces
still forming,
heads slightly out of round,

singing "I Gave My Love
A Cherry,"
or "Big Rock Candy Mountain."

There was the recital
we never gave
because, to tell the truth,

we weren't very good.
One boy is dead
now, three are welders,

two joined the Navy, one
sells used cars,
half a dozen are farmers,

one has been convicted
of exporting
Nazi literature to Germany.

I don't remember any of us
as mortal
or talented or cruel.

All we ever learned was that
chord progression,
knowable and sequential —

beautiful as gears shifting —
something useful
and at the bottom of all

the music we imagined we
could care about.
We knew who Mozart was

but there wasn't any Mozart
for the ukulele.
That would have been wrong

and we knew it — some of us.
Or none
of us. Either way.

Keith Ratzlaff

— *after Christopher Smart*

For I will consider my cat Nell.
For in winter she is a hunch of fur wrapped around herself.
For Venetian blinds their dusty ladders up and down.
For autumn's ambiguity gone, summer's green
      which was deception.
For the window which is not servile
      which doesn't care what you see.
For inline skates or out.
For a boy on the sidewalk this morning, skating.
For February's gruel-like sun, starlings in the bony maple
      their teal sheen and squawking.
For their cocky lift of wings.
For their croaking which is rasps grinding rasps.

My cat is autumn mottled, brown for sincerity, orange for not,
      gold flecks for not.
Out the window, a boy skating, confident
      in the wheels and laces and balance.
Which is the prerogative of the upright.
Which is spirit over dross.
Which is a boy helmeted just in case for his mother
      but who eschews kneepads for recklessness and for himself.
For he is a mixture of gravity and waggery.
For he has pulled the prank of peeing in his brother's bed.
Prank upon prank for which he deserves a hiding.
For hiding--which is skin and concealment, outside and in,
      the beating and what's being beaten.
For he is hated by his brother every other day.
For he hath put sawdust in the fish food again.
For this morning he will fall for no better reason than he should.

And watching him is like watching myself.
As if this were news, the pang of my nevermore self,

the old man I almost am.
For the orange I ate this morning, stinging and clear.
For mild February, the ice on the pond
        not thick enough to hold us.
For our weight upon the earth.
For my mother's friend, whom Parkinson's disease has killed.
For his intellect which was a spirit
        trapped in an earthquaked house.
For Parkinson's disease, its trembling and shuffle,
        its cage and canary.
For the relief he obtained from dopamine.
For my mother's voice, which is too matter-of-fact about this.
For the brain cells of fetuses.
For all the things I wish there were another way to say.

For Parkinson's which my friend Alex doth put to sleep
        with a tumbler of scotch.
For scotch upon scotch in which I would join him
        until we are singing show tunes.
For ice on the pond or no ice on the pond.
For the rat that bites our throat.
For doe a female deer.
For fear that is expectation and fear that is resignation.
For the boy beginning his descent, in the throes of falling.
For my mother, her wish never to reach ninety: "Oh I don't
        want to ever make it that far," she said.
She said to me.
Who is docile and can learn certain things.
Who once tried to light an ice cube with a match.
Who has never considered her life, how she might regret it,
        how we tire of the wax and fire of the body.

For irony which is like a joyful noise.
For whistling a happy tune.
For the boy I never was.

For the Lord God is good, his mercy endureth.
For a skating boy falling, who wants no part of mercy
        but who covets the everlasting courts of praise.
Who wants to be good but who is really a creep.
Who is falling, flapping like the earth's last bird,
        fluttering, shaking, speaking the electrical language
        of prayer as he falls.
For almost, which is the treading of water.
For the moment — this one — which hangs on like drifts
        in the house's north shadow.
For longing, which is the arrow of regret.
For regret, for not now, not yet.

HOWLING DOG

Keith Ratzlaff

This is a poem for Max,
my neighbor's Husky,
howling at the snow drifts
at the orange-lit sky.
His chest is a squeeze-box
under the evening spruce,
under the moon's white hieroglyph.

And I'm howling, too,
because I'm a little drunk,
because it's cold,
because I'm carrying
a bucket of parings
to the frozen compost pile.
Because Max is keening
from a low throat churn
up three dog octaves
and down again, a country song
kind of howl-oh honey
you done broke my heart
just bury it in the yard.

He's a sweet dog, really,
but he's been chained
to the garage so long —
four years? five?
dog years beyond counting —
he's now unfit for children
or the farm. One day
he'll make a break for it
and not come back for all
the usual car-struck,
bulleted, packdog reasons.

So he's a good old dog
who will never not be chained,
governed by the old laws
of territory and possession,
wall and radius, driveway
and food and misdirected love.
My wife has volunteered
to walk him, teach him
emancipation means literally
to be led by the hand —
which means leash,
which means collar
he'll have none of.

There's no villain here.
Not Max's first owner
who shot himself. Not
my neighbor who loves
Max and everything
in the world so much
he can't let them go.
Not Max himself who
imitates the semis
that drive him crazy,
shifting gears —
4th 5th 7th 11th —
(shut the goddamned dog up,
someone yells in the dark)
until he's calling like
a muezzin to the angels —
arch angels and thrones
virtues, powers, dominations —
God's dogs shackled
to God's garage
on short chains, too.

Who do what they're told:
go and sit, stay and heel,
who wait for the biscuit
on the nose trick,
that humiliation.
But God is good, really,
we've settled that old issue.
He has made us a little
lower than the angels,
but hears us when we howl.
He knows our songs
are equal parts
lying and heartbreak,
lawlessness and praise —
un- and mild-mannered,
tethered and wagging,
bad dogs, good dogs
that we are.

RECOGNITION OF THE MATE

Sherry Rind

When the sun travels a certain perimeter
in our sky — and no one knows what it is —
causing light to fall
at a particular angle where it meets
a sensory point on the frog's head
the frog, let us say the *Hyla regilla*
moves downhill to his accustomed
breeding pond as surely as a salmon
finds the way to its birth stream
and at dusk he forces air back and forth
across his vocal cords
producing his characteristic song
thus enticing the female
from her hiding place until she comes near
enough for him to clasp her
and not let go until she lays her eggs.

The point of similarity
is the path created in the brain
that leads one to another
by instinct in frogs and, in us, by a learned
response that began, 1 believe,
when I first saw you and liked your color
as you, perhaps, liked my shape —
note that the male frog recognizes the female
by her shape. This first nerve impulse
was reinforced by repeated sightings,
sounds, and touch until your presence
became in me a place to inhabit
as I inhabit my home
or the frog, his breeding pool.

Further study is needed to determine
the point at which we chose
to go on deepening, by repetition, the path
in our bodies and brains,
the point at which we could have stopped
and let go of each other without
damaging the delicate fibers
of our arms and legs and mouths and nerves
but I do know absolutely, my love,
that at this point I
will allow no letting go.

EGGS OF THE RED-LEGGED FROG

Sherry Rind

a silk purseful
of green grapes
or the crackling clear vinyl
coin purses maiden great aunts carried
filled with pennies and dimes
and a five dollar bill
and gold cased lipstick
and cloudy barley sugar candies
wrapped in limp cellophane

or periods turning to commas
pointing back the way we came
but we must go forward
fertilized or not
mated or single

with the daily struggle to produce
functional arms and legs and lungs
being at first
the size of the second fingernail
on a dainty woman's hand
we beach
hoping to survive
our own good luck

A WINDOW IN THE ROOF

Sherry Rind

Down to us sky spread
its flat blue hands
where we lay, eyes open to stars,
recording the passing lights
of each season: grey dawn or blue,
low sun, red moon.

I floated all night in the empty
turning of the planet
with no dreams but those of stars
travelling away for no particular reason.
Sometimes at dinner I stopped
mid-sentence, watching the dark
open on the table cloth — space
with no atoms to carry sound.

Facing every night
air mass and cloud,
the invisible debris of dead planets,
here and here we lay
in the random juxtaposition of two stars.
I began to dream you were another life
I had left.

The man on the late news tells me
a radioactive cloud from a bomb test in China
is floating overhead.
I open the window to get it over with

and wait for the moment of clarity
when the order and purpose of my life
will spread before me like a set table
in the Neiman-Marcus catalogue,
when my attempts to rise early,
hold a steady job, remember the Sabbath,
and maintain the animal order of life
to enrich my soul and lighten my disposition
will all make sense.

This time there's no use calling Mother
to ask how she is and stave off
her death from grief. This time
there's even no use being Jewish.
I am tired of trying to be good.
I am ready to give myself up.

Breathing bus exhaust
I survey my last view of the city
its buildings like upright citizens
its freeway with no beginning or end.
Across the street a stranger leans out
as if she, too, is waiting for the dust.
We wave forgiveness at each other.
The dust, the reporter says,
will not fall on us this time.

Sherry Rind

Pure, or basic, research, in the jargon of science, is work so fundamental that no one can yet see how the results might have any practical value.
— *James Trefil, Robinson Professor of Physics, George Mason University*

The sun is not matter as you and I know it
but dust and gas balanced
between the outward pulse of burning hydrogen
and inward press of gravity, temporarily
stable.

>   *Stable*, a place to house a horse
>   where heat and cold penetrate equally,
>   where sunlight angles against dust motes
>   and turns them gold
>   and the smell of horse sweat
>   burns in women until they radiate love.

For an eternity, as only we know it,
the sun will burn hotter
until it boils away the oceans
and all water-dependent
life.

>   *Life*, a place in time
>   with beginning and end
>   like a story, like us
>   and mayflies, elephants
>   and the sun, which began
>   4.5 billion years ago.

Given 11 billion years, the sun
will burn itself up and display in space,
collapsing and swelling, hissing and spitting
in nuclear action-reaction like a galactic
courtship dance.

Courtship behavior in birds is chemically
determined: the peacock does not think
to raise his multicolored fan; the urge
simply kicks at the sight of a hen
in March, but the everlasting mystery
is why this hen and not the other.

One last contraction will leave the sun
a white dwarf, slowly leaking heat onto dead planets
until it turns across earth's horizon
with no light at all in a lightless
sky.

> *Sky,* the place without
> conceivable end, where children
> see God, where we look daily
> to orient ourselves in time
> and see birds rise out of sight.

In first light the desert horned lizard
warms itself, its pineal eye
monitoring the balance of heat and shade
to maintain its intricate relationship with
the sun.

> *Sun,* with a lifespan extending beyond
> imagination into faith,
> sends heat we compare to love,
> measuring our courtships
> in a daily circuit, the impervious
> clock of our beginning and end.

A horned lizard will flatten on your palm
where your blood becomes its life-giving heat
and you can stroke its small, sharp horns,
creating a communion as mortal
as sunrise.

Sherry Rind

I apologize for sending you this poem
botched with bird droppings. Usually
I am careful to keep the parrot away
from the desk but, as Grandpa said,
you know how it is. Accidents happen
before we know they have begun.

News on my desk includes the birth
of a straw-colored fruit bat
whose mother rejects her young
at two weeks of age. Does she forget
they are hers? Tire of their hunger?
How many repetitions make a habit?

Imagine taking home a fruit bat to nurse,
hooking it on the curtain rod
with an old towel as surrogate mother
and a pile of newspaper below.
Its cries of greeting would be barely perceptible.
Who knows what other messages you would miss?

The sky's clutter stacks into orderly strata
from stars to crows, the road crew
who eat snakes and scatter debris for the ants.
Somewhere beneath the correspondence,
poems, notes, and impossible requests for money
hides Grandpa's solid oak desk

colored now like a copper plate etched
with generations of black scribblings
accounting our lives into habit and accident
as he counted debits and credits.
I would like to clear this desk.
I would like us to come clean.

FOOD CHAIN

Sherry Rind

A scat study of wild snow leopards yielded the following annual menu per animal: five blue sheep, five domestic goats, one domestic sheep, marmots, nine Tibetan woolly hare, fifteen birds.
— R.S. Chundawat, Snow Line, Vol. XI, No. 1, 1993.

How many marmots?
Are they insignificant
or numberless like stars?
Humble, rounded rodents
of earth's upper crust
they whistle an evensong
peak to peak.
The end of the day is coming,
the end, they say,
and the blue sheep
raise their heads from scrubby grass
and know it is time
to hide from leopards.

By tens and fifteens
marmots heap into burrows
for winter, squeezing past
and over each other,
casting pink litters
like grains of rice.
Biologists count all the snow leopards
in the world,
the number of goats in Tibet,
even the number of days
in one life.

They must guess at marmots
whose numbers ebb and flow
as seamlessly as seasons,
who sleep inside the earth
but are plucked like flowers
from the mountainside,
who know by shade of sky
and weight of air
that day is closing.
Then they sing.

LETTER FROM HOME

Yvonne Sapia

Hija mia,
Creo que
La Muerte te cogio
o El Amor te encontro

Received the money order
but no reply
to my last letters.
You must not have much to say.

Mother's heart is better
though still cold to me.
But to our old aunts,
she suffers like a saint.

Father's fish stories
have foundered.
No one believes him
about lures anymore.

Together, they are like
two gray statues
in the empty fountain
across from City Hall.

A neighbor is baking bread.
The aroma comes through
the house as darkness comes.
There is so little daylight left.

Tomorrow I will take my bag
and walk down to Calle Ocho.
I must occupy my mind
until you visit me.

Until you visit me
I must rake the leaves
and beat the rugs
and change the tablecloth;

then listen from my room
to the boarder and his company
turn in the bed at night
and turn the night in bed.

FERTILE CRESCENT

Yvonne Sapia

The shallow arms of the river caress my house.
I am the washerwoman pounding
a futile vision against the rocks.
I wash my clothes in the river's importance.

I've seen dark men walk the banks
of this river. They have waited in moonlight
drenched in that sound of water,
shoulders up against the cold currents.

The lizards have made violent love
by the river beneath a brief sun.
I've watched the perfect lovers
rolling on their green, jagged backs.

The river carries ceremonies and dreams.
In the night I draw a swollen moon
into my mouth and turn
to the river going under.

Into the black offering I fall like a millstone;
into forgetfulness I go further down.
The ocean celebrates my coming
with the vernacular of sea gulls.

Yvonne Sapia

when the river
first gave birth
to itself
the crops were flooded

like misguided pharaohs
the haggard men waded
through new river

each year that followed
the river overflowed
and they celebrated
like egyptians
like slaves to the river

they called the river by name
sang to it
while in it
soaked their legs
washed their hair
in the river

it ran through them
with its plain thought
the waters became
their thoughts

they slept
through flooded nights
while waters pronounced
their names
and the river pronounced
its own name
a word made of water

bobbing at dry edges
of dreams

but one fastidious year
the river did not return

a silent hypocrite
the slowly dying river
slothed out of their arms

farmers stood in the reeds
speaking to each other
with hard eyes
as icons of jesus and john wayne
floated away

ENGLISH ONLY!

Yvonne Sapia

for all who learned to speak again

the salesman shouts at my old aunts who cluck
in Spanish like three lost chickens at his
counter in the mall on Martin Luther

King Day. They think a piece of jewelry
is *bonito* for a niece in P.R.
Yet he wishes to keep pure a language

that long ago lost innocence and stole
from every tongue one time or another.
"Is that your hair?" he asks me, not knowing

the electric shock look is natural
for the women in our tribe. "Are they black
or white?" (I am glad my aunts do not speak

English.) "Both," I say and pay the hateful
price they've paid since leaving the island to
be told they are never to utter words

like "*Que pasa?*" or "*Hasta la vista,*
baby!" Or to simply say, *"No."* But which
of the No's? The Spanish No brandished like

a knife? Universal No's immigrant
grandparents wailed? Or muffled No's of those
unable to speak with their tongues cut out?

THESE ARE MY GHOSTS

Yvonne Sapia

1.

Move close to me in this new light
so I may see your eyes again.
I then may comprehend the night.
Move close to me in this new light.
Where are you now? I hear the slight
breathing of one who is broken.
Move close to me in this new light
so I may see your eyes again.

2.

You turn to smoke beneath the trees.
How do I know you will come back
to me as before? With such ease
you turn to smoke. Beneath the trees
I cross your path, your mystery
intriguing as the twigs that crack.
You turn to smoke beneath the trees.
How do I know you will come back?

3.

Your burden is that you are lost
in between two sleeping lovers.
They cannot recognize your ghost.
Their burden is that they are lost.
Tombstones are covered hard with frost.
Above the dead ones, night hovers.
Your burden is that you are lost
in between two sleeping lovers.

4.
Take my soul like an opened eye.
I need to see what you have seen.
Even if the vision horrifies,
take my soul. Like an opened eye,
I witness but don't know I lie
in order to believe my dream.
Take my soul like an opened eye.
I need to see what you have seen.

STAR DEATH

Yvonne Sapia

Five billion summers
from today,

our sun will burn out.
It will sit

in a cloud of gas
like a red

giant emblazoned
by comets.

Condensation and
stellar winds,

in spectacular
fashion, will

spread from its center
until, with

unprecedented
clarity,

its image dies off.
Cold with this

calling, our last words
will brush their

soft lips against us
all night long.

THE ROSES

Ruth L. Schwartz

for Mark Doty

During that time before the surgery,
I wandered through half-shattered greenhouses,
a holocaust of roses. Thousands and thousands of them
yanked up with tractors, the wide thornless knobs of root-ball
scattered in the dirt like small lost skulls —
and their millions of blossoms wilting at once,
the lights of each of their petals shuddering
like the end of the world.
And it took weeks, the wrecking of everything,
so we went once with gloves and a bucket;
G. was weak already, her skin grayish as toast
which was all she ate, those nausea-ruled days,
but we took as many as we could.
They won't live outside the greenhouse,
someone told me; but he lied,
there are twelve of them blooming now in our yard.
Twelve. A small tribunal of survivors.

Imagine this, Mark. If you could have saved the man you loved.
If someone could have cut you open, removed
what he needed, sewn it into him.
Imagine that weight you called *relentless,* his flesh
retrieved; his perfect chin against your collarbone, forehead
to your lips, his body
in a kind of miracle stasis,
as if all the oceans of the world had been caught and held
just at the crest of a vast wave
before it bucked and crashed and broke, flooding everything ...

The shamans say each organ has a soul.
The doctors only know it works:
the kidney they cut from my arteries, attached to hers,
which took just two heartbeats' time

to make some urine in her, squirt it out
onto the hospital floor
like a new baby.
Months later, I still startle at the red healed rivers
of our scars; I still wonder where love comes from
when it pours from us like this, in spite of everything —
and how the universe can catch and hold it and make use of it
as it flows by the lips of those
it cannot save, flows over

HIEROGLYPHICS
ON A BRANCH OF PEACH

Ruth L. Schwartz

for Shari

Once, a woman made love to me
through the slippery dark.
Her brother was dying, her sisters were shooting
heroin in the bathroom as she moved her tongue
like sadness on my skin, and I felt
how all the sweet explosions —
summer, orgasm, a ripe peach in the mouth —
connect unfailingly to the barren fields.

What we have learned about love in this life
can never be removed from us.
Not one minute pried
from any of the days —
and yet, there was a worm
which entered the live branch,

lived and ate and tunneled through
the wooden heart, and with its body wrote
new language
through the lost years.

So there must be another,
more convincing name for innocence,
the kind the body never lost,
the grace of stumbling
through an open door —

Ruth L. Schwartz

after Rilke

> A 13-year-old Oakland boy was robbed at gunpoint in the
> stairway of his middle school ... for his new $140 Nike shoes.
> — *San Francisco Chronicle*

The pink camellia, blooming face down to the ground, in the
      battering rain —
which is the body, all its fragmented unfurling, prayer and longing
      wasted, trapped.
Robbed at gunpoint in the stairwell of his junior high, the 13-year-old
who'd worked for months of weekends, reports the newspaper,
selling roses and incense, in an Oakland parking lot,
earning the money for those shoes ...
Listen, if there were no guns,
if there were no billion-dollar advertising budgets,
if there were no far-off factories, filled with fifty-cents-an-hour workers,
if we had not been suckled on despair and greed,
if even two people could live together, side by side, at peace with self
      and other,
if we were not, at the same time, cowering behind bitter masks,
if the camellia had not bloomed today, beneath such rain,
if the bush had held more firmly to the twig, gripping the open pinkness
      of the face, now crushed
into the concrete stubble,
if we had never stopped to buy those roses, that incense, which promised to
      sweeten our nights,
if the boy, now stumbling to his bare feet in the stairwell,
did not long less for his sneakers than for revenge,
if the spirit trapped inside the earth could break
the walls of every one of us, opening and filling us
with wisdom and light,

            would we change our lives?

FLAMENCO GUITAR

Ruth L. Schwartz

This music is the country you lost
when you were born,
the cafe which never closes, the sex which
comes so close your pores are
weeping with longing, and never touches you,
the nights you don't sleep, the hands in their ceaseless
moving like birds, the conversations interrupted
only by dancing, the dancers weeping with their bodies
painted like eyes,
here where black coffee and red wine are the only
waters, where crusty bread and creamy cheese
flecked with oregano and pooling tears of olive oil
are the only foods.
It's the music you strain to hear through all the needy
ordinary days,
the music which will only stop
when you abandon everything to follow it
— because this music lies to you, but it's a gorgeous lie,
full of such craving and entreaty, the chance for nothing
to be ordinary, ever.

It's like Conrad's heart of darkness, says the guitarist
later, when you introduce yourself
and learn he has a day job, he's a psychologist,
this isn't Seville, just College Avenue in Oakland,
the passions so much larger than our bodies
are lodged in our bodies, there is nothing we can do
to be rid of them, not the passions, not the bodies,
because whatever you make of your life
the soul keeps turning the other way,
like a child leaning backwards
over a railing toward the water, hanging by its feet,

so this music which is motion itself, you want it
to hold still,
its frenzy fixed so you can look
through its violet scarlet tangerine lens —

and glimpse your life there, floating in the colors

IMPORTANT THING

Ruth L. Schwartz

I've always loved the way pelicans dive,
as if each silver fish they see
were the goddamned most important
thing they've ever wanted on this earth —
and just tonight I learned sometimes
they go blind doing it,
that straight-down dive like someone jumping
from a rooftop, only happier,
plummeting like Icarus, but more triumphant —
      there is the undulating fish,
        the gleaming sea,
there is the chance to taste again
the kind of joy which can be eaten whole,
and this is how they know to reach it,
head-first, high-speed, risking everything,

          and some of the time they come back up
as if it were nothing, they bob on the water,
silver fish like stogies angled
rakishly in their wide beaks,
— then the enormous
          stretching of the throat,
then the slow unfolding
          of the great wings,
as if it were nothing, sometimes they do this
a hundred times or more a day,
as long as they can see, they rise
        back into the sky
to begin again —

        and when they can't?

We know, of course, what happens,
they starve to death, not a metaphor, not a poem in it;

this goes on every day of our lives,
and the man whose melting wings
spatter like a hundred dripping candles
                    over everything,

and the suicide who glimpses, in the final
seconds of her fall,
        all the other lives she might have lived.

                The ending doesn't have to be happy.
                The hunger itself is the thing.

Ruth L. Schwartz

Nothing is ever too hard for a dog,
all big dumb happiness and effort.
This one keeps swimming out into the
icy water for a stick,
he'd do it all day and all night
if you'd throw it that long,
he'd do it till it killed him, then he'd die
dripping and shining, a black waterfall,
the soggy broken stick still clenched
in his doggy teeth,

and watching him you want to cry
for all the wanting you've forsworn,
and how, when he hits deeper water,
his body surges suddenly, as if to say
Nothing could stop me now —
while you're still thinking everything
you've ever loved
meant giving up some other thing you loved,
your hand, the stick stuck in the air,
in the shining air.

AIDS EDUCATION, SEVENTH GRADE

Ruth L. Schwartz

— for Mark Montoya

This poem follows the sequence of the three-day AIDS education program provided in many Bay Area schools.

Day One — AIDS Overview
The children are blooming like black flowers,
their teeth are white and lovely, it doesn't matter
what country they live in, the dying
moves over them like wind
through the captured fields.
When I ask how many know someone with AIDS
they all shout, their arms rising like snakes,
waving hungry palms,
Can a dog get it, can you get it from a hickey,
why can't they just pump out all a person's blood
and put in new?
Afterward the teacher says to me, That one there,
buck teeth, she has sex with three or four boys a week,
they come over from the high school,
do it to her in the yard,
her sister had a baby at thirteen —
and overhead, the dark
bodies of the hawks
riding their hunger through the clear sky,
the sun laying its fair, long tongue
over everything.

Day Two — A Speaker With AIDS
One-third of the class speaks no English
and Mark of the beautiful Indian cheekbones,
the barrio, the broken, winged life
stumbles in his grandparents' Spanish

so the solemn little freckled kid translates
as Mark says, Tell them it's going to kill me,
saying, *Dice que le va a matar,*
his dark-lashed sunflower face composed,

and the sun says, Forget about the forty days
and nights of rain, I'm here, I'm burning.

Day Three — You Must Protect Yourself
It's like shouting from the shore
of a glittering lake,
Look, we've been given these bodies
we don't understand,
we could spend our whole lives
learning how to live in them.

It doesn't matter what I say.

Sex, if it hasn't already, will rise up in them
like something from another world,
like the snowy egret on its perfect stilts
in the dank puddle by the highway,
shocking in its grace,
fishing for its life

STOPPING BY WENATCHEE ON THE WAY
TO SEE SOMEPLACE ELSE

Julianne Seeman

down Stevens Pass
the Wenatchee River cascades
over fists of white rock and
settles in brown hills
where irrigation sprinklers
pump like a heart
across the orchards

my children are silent
even in town this is August
in the backseat crush
of camping gear
and these are my landmarks:
the pool and skating rink,
the Owl Drug, Cascadian Hotel,
the Burke Hill Apartments,
the Plaza,
and across the street
beside cannon in the park
the old men still
playing checkers

when the street forks up the hill
I know the way
under tents of elms and maples
past my mother's high school
then left down Idaho
where the house stands still and
white beside the Dead End sign
I say here is the swing
my grandfather hung
and this is the wall he built
this is the porch

where my grandmother stood
these are the rooms
I was as small as you

we were all as small
as you

that was an orchard
there was dust
and the high sweet smell of cots
in the August burn
the houses are new
but this is the time it takes
to graft a tree

this is how you climb
this is the fruit
pick it clean

Julianne Seeman

— for Linda

Here time is measured in weather
the cracked lines on faces
and the lives of women buried
on these plains: their stories the rib
lines of work and loss, dreams hard
as fenceposts;
acres of wire and the bawl of calves,
rolls of summer
wheat heaped like amber fists.
Inside the *Cozy Corner*, we order
steak and fries, hot apple pie and listen
to the low tide of voices,
fourth generation ranchers,
the soft chant of survival:
this stock, that price, boards
peeling back to grey; and down the road
another man pulls out: no water,
hired hands quit, the combine breaks
down again. But here the low ebb of sun
burns the tensile surface of Lake Petroleum,
my kayak glides like breath,
the dogs race along the shore —
and I understand why
you had to come home.

AT THE SHELDON JACKSON MUSEUM

Julianne Seeman

In the solemn glow
of amber light
and Plexiglas, silence
deep as arctic
winter, soft as sun
on birch , we move
from scene to scene
that show us how
they lived
until they perished
at the hands of Russian traders
who stole their furs
and wives and left behind
their Christian God, Small Pox
and rot-gut whiskey lining
Third Avenue where they wander
from bar to bar searching
for home. What was left
is in this careful
room: temperature
controlled, light subdued
on seal gut suits
luminous as skin, stitched
with sea grass, water tight
as kayaks strong enough
to carry men across
the swollen seas hunting
seal and whale.
Imagine these small rooms
lit by oil light, fires burning,
women's laughter soft
as infant's cooing, men
bursting through the door
arms laden. Imagine all this
then imagine silence
like a prayer

CORDOVA, AUGUST, 1992

Julianne Seeman

This was someone's dream,
this bleached out row boat
seeded with fireweed, scruff grass
and willow, parked now in a vacant lot
beside the peeling clapboard exterior
of the Alaskan Hotel,
a block from Obstruction Point,
where tourists can look out
to mountains raising blue fists
from Prince William Sound,
clean on the surface, but under rocks
crude oil still
they can't get off. Never mind
what they say. Above the cove,
red long johns flap
against metallic sky.
Out on the Copper River Road
the Million Dollar bridge twists
in Arctic wind. The earthquake
broke the bridge in '64,
but Child's Glacier moans
beneath steel light where Trumpeter Swans
glide still as Eyak spirits. What is left
survives in books where we wait out the storm
in sagging chairs beneath florescent light
that sears this room silent as a church.
Across from me a fisherman thumbs *Newsweek,*
dripping rain and loneliness. Out on the street
the hotel sign hangs upside down
so drunks can see where they are
in the morning. On either side
of smoke-stained glass
shoulders line the longest bar in Alaska.
Next door, the broken window
looks like a falling star.

TAKING DOWN THE ARBOR

Julianne Seeman

— for Linda

Rickey's arbor, you say
announcing our task again
after I haul the ladder and shovel
up from the orchard, and we have searched
the shed for the 15 millimeter socket,
found the ratchet and wrench.
We knock off the cross bars
then you bump me aside,
climb the precarious steps and
wedge your body against the bolt:
Left loose; right tight. Isn't
that what you told me?
Sounds of traffic,
the close smell of rain, the bay
a steel light beyond the orchard,
heavy with apples and pears. April nuzzles
the fence, the dogs stretch on the cool grass
watching. One end of the first beam
drops down.

Rickey's memorial arbor, you say,
your voice caressing the name
you called him the last weeks of his life.
It will go into my yard
to frame the grapes you planted there
last spring.
Next summer, you will sell this place
move to Montana.
But first the arbor he built five years

before January sun polished
the grey tangle of Wisteria. Twelve foot
four by fours solid as the day he set them
two feet down. I dig at the base,
rock the first one loose and together we lift,
leaning into the weight,
pull each one free
from the ground.

Hal Shows

1

Foreign arpeggio of pelican and gull.
The sea continues to crash
Against
The solid world,
This arching dune,
The vacant boardwalk three miles off.
Penelope's weaving is undone,
A wave breaks across the empty shore:
Smoke on a ceiling.
Glass
Shattered. Thin fingers touching a face.

2
Trough of Sandpiper,
Lifeline of Glistening Fish,
The slough
Connects the sea
And the steaming tidepool,
Becoming
A black runout
In the whitewater.

I bend
To uncover a conch shell in the mud,
Whorled like a delicate ear.
Deeper and deeper
The pink bands sink
To the blood-red center of the cone.
I stand

Still, to listen.
Wherever I walk,
My footsoles crack the shells
Of the dead,
Starfish,
Anemone, putrid remains
Of catfish and shark,
Ground down to similar sand.

3

Why praise the change, if change is all we know?
What roots and worm and the mistletoe?
The moon on water will buckle and break

On a wave; why praise the change?
If the oceans boil, and vanish, the moon remains.
What hopes to last must undergo its end,

Collapse, fall, and feed a newer bloom.
The trawler's winch is rusted, the groundswell
                                        rolls,
Waves break, the sun and moon descend,
The silkworm knits the moon to the mistletoe.

4

Mired, sodden but upward-straining, the wings
    of a bird
Burst the bindings of the book of myth
Flail the air
Out of the conch shell's hidden core
In long gusts against my eardrum.
Between the wave breaking itself into infinity,
And the sloped dune that does not break,
But is slowly leveled.
Conch shells are made,
Fragile, wave-shaped cisterns
Housing whatever the whitewater breaks,
Wells of flux, drowning
The bitter, deluded shards of permanence.
A voice that is my voice, or my voice
    becoming
The voice of another,
Effortless cadenza of sand the craftsman
Carving crescents and ridges into the back of a shell,
Refuses the frozen Eternity of Heaven,
Chooses to hold what comes and goes, breaking
Its own bones over and over to finest dust.

5

If my voice grafts to itself the cadence
Of ridges and whorls,

If my bones open to the song
Of a drowned man,

Who, sinking,
Sang his crown of barnacles

Into a wreath of poppies and roses,
What have I learned?

To build, and let go?
To hold

The conch shell to my ear,
To lift my head upward into infinite air?

Hal Shows

"Every scene must further the plot," and so on.
But I was thinking of a fine, ghostwritten film
subtle as any of the tales my grandmother told.
Maybe it made the papers; here is its gist:
a west-ender heads east, with a vast wardrobe.
After the disastrously comic lateness of the train
he arrives in colonial pomp but is unreceived.
He feels like a lost bag in the empty station.

What makes the movie is the fact he finds a home.
Half-starved, always hauling his half-digested
European baggage around, he sheds himself.
Skins later he's given away his tailored clothes,
has grown sane and lustrous in the long dusk,
and all the explosive natives take him to heart.

Hal Shows

Lovers come and lovers go,
attired in ever-starchier garments of regret,
finally they flee through the pines and fade,
in the dying light.

Alone, I rehearse that passion.
I hear the same hushed voice insisting,
suffer the same silvery rush to abandon my clothes.
A lion, I am lifted by lips.
On fragrant shields of skin I am offered to the sun.
I stammer the same hurt curses
in the lengthening night.

It is fall, it is truly fall in the world,
last call for the senses,
a season of knife-like sight.
Short and cool, the kind days
keep the marshy smell of sex fresh on my fingers
from bath to bath, from dark to dark,
through wrong and right.

DAY BEGINS AT
GOVERNOR'S SQUARE MALL

Leon Stokesbury

Here, newness is all. Or almost all. And like
a platterful of pope's noses at a White House dinner,
I exist apart. But these trees now —
how do you suppose they grow this high in here?
They look a little like the trees I sat beneath in 1959
waiting with my cheesecloth net for butterflies.
It was August and it was hot. Late summer,
yes, but already the leaves in trees were
flecked with ochers and the umbers of the dead.
I sweated there for hours, so driven,
so immersed in the forest's shimmering life,
that I could will my anxious self not move
for half a day — just on the imagined chance
of making some slight part of it my own.
Then they came. One perfect pair of just-hatched
black-and-white striped butterflies. The white
lemon-tipped with light, in shade
then out, meandering. Zebra swallowtails,
floating, drunk in the sun, so rare to find
their narrow, fragile, two-inch tails intact.
At that moment I could only drop my net and stare.
The last of August. 1959. But these trees, now,
climb up through air and concrete never hot or cold.
And I suspect the last lepidoptera that found
themselves in here were sprayed then swept away.
Everyone is waiting though, as before a storm —
anticipating something. Do these leaves never fall?

Now, and with a mild surprise, faint
music falls. But no shop breaks open yet.
The people, like myself, range aimlessly;
the air seems thick and still. Then, lights blink on;
the escalators jerk and hum. And in the center, at
the exact center of the mall, a jet of water spurts

twenty feet straight up, then drops and spatters
in a shallow pool where signs announce that none
may ever go. O bright communion! O new cathedral!
where the appetitious, the impure, the old, the young,
the bored, the lost, the dumb, with wide dilated eyes
advance with offerings to be absolved and be made clean.
Now, the lime-lit chainlink fronts from over one hundred
modern and convenient stalls and stores are rolled away.
Now, odors of frying won tons come wafting up from
Lucy Ho's Bamboo Garden. And this music, always
everywhere, yet also somehow strangely played as if
not to be heard, pours its soft harangue down now.
The people wander forward now. And the world begins.

UNSENT MESSAGE
TO MY BROTHER IN HIS PAIN

Leon Stokesbury

Please do not die now. Listen.
Yesterday, storm clouds rolled
out of the west like thick muscles.
Lightning bloomed. Such a sideshow
of colors. You should have seen it.
A woman watched with me, then we slept.
Then, when I woke first, I saw
in her face that rest is possible.
The sky, it suddenly seems
important to tell you, the sky
was pink as a shell. Listen
to me. People orbit the moon now.
They must look like flies around
Fatty Arbuckle's head, that new
and that strange. My fellow American,
I bought a French cookbook. In it
are hundreds and hundreds of recipes.
If you come to see me, I shit you not,
we will cook with wine. Listen
to me. Listen to me, my brother,
please don't go. Take a later flight,
a later train. Another look around.

LISTENING TO MY MOTHER'S COMIC BANTER WITH SACKBOYS AND SERVERS

Leon Stokesbury

It is in brief moments such as these
that I know there is no god.
And I do not suppose that,
in even one of her seventy-
some-odd years, it has entered
my mother's mind that the look
in this young man's eyes, adrift
somewhere between shock and shame,
might ever be anything except
kindred and reciprocal laughter.
In his attempts at ascertaining
her desire to supersize her fries
or seeing her apples and Oreos
safely stowed, the server seems
caught off guard, and vaguely amazed
by my mother's grins and gab.
She, however, sees only a co-
conspirator, one who also gets
the joke with no name, her palaver
often beginning with something
along the lines of "working hard,"
then straight to "hardly working." Then,
if she perceives what she conceives
to be consent, the proper glance
or repartee, silence giving consent,
it eggs her on to escalate to snickers,
then, perhaps, to "Lord, it's hot! I'm
just a-sweatin!" Graduating quick
enough from there to comments
maybe on the constant rise in
costs of things: "Shit fire to save
matches!" and beyond. Now, I

have borne witness to this bizarre
ascension many times. And always
at its end, I observe my mother's eyes
shifting from her daily dull to a fine
acetylene shine: opaque proof, at
best, of linkage to some living
thing outside herself. For
long ago I think somehow
my mother must have caught
a glimpse of some immense
and empty ought, some vacant
maw. And although she never
said so, would not even know
how to say so, it seems that,
ever since that time, she reaches
out to any sign, relying even on
the fantasized response of this
poor teenaged boy, as some bleak
buffer piled against confronting
that sad chasm once again, any
line to keep that zap of night
at bay, depending on any bray
of mindless blather, his requesting
now her preference for paper
over plastic, lilt, any semblance
of communion, the kindness
of strangers on any blessed day.

Leon Stokesbury

For the first time in what must be
the better part of two years now
I happened to hear Janis
in her glory —
all that tinctured syrup
dripping off
a razorblade —
on the radio today singing "Summertime."

And it took me back to this girl I knew,
a woman really, my first year
writing undergraduate poetry
at the Mirabeau B. Lamar
State College of Technology
in Beaumont, Texas,
back in 1966.

This woman was the latest in a line,
the latest steady
of my friend John Coyle that spring —
and I remember she was plain:
she was short: and plain
and wore her brown hair up
in a sort of bun in back
that made her plainer still.

I don't know where John met her,
but word went round
she had moved back in with Mom and Dad
down in Port Arthur
to get her head straight,
to attend Lamar,
to study History,

after several years in San Francisco
where she had drifted
into a "bad scene"
taking heroin.

I was twenty,
still lived with Mom and Dad myself,
and so knew nothing
about "bad scenes,"
but I do remember once or twice
each month that spring
John would give a party
with this woman always there.
And always as the evening's end came on
this woman, silent for hours,
would reveal, from thin air,
her guitar,
settle in a chair,
release her long hair
from the bun it was in,
and begin.

Her hair flowed over her shoulders,
and the ends of the strands of hair
like tarnished brass in lamplight
would brush and drag across
the sides of the guitar
as this woman bent
over it.

How low and guttural, how
slow and torchlit, how
amber her song, how absolutely
unlike the tiny nondescript

a few minutes before.
And I remember also,
from later on that spring,
from May of that year,
two nights in particular.

The first night was a party
this woman gave
at her parents' home.
Her parents' home
was beige:
the bricks the parents' home
was built with
were beige.
The entire house was carpeted
in beige.

John's girl greeted everyone at the door,
a martini in one hand
and a lit cigarette
in an Oriental
ivory cigarette holder in the other,
laughing
for once, and tossing back
her long brown hair.

All the women wore
black full-length party dresses —
and I remember the young woman's father,
how odd he seemed
in his charcoal suit and tie,
his gray hair —
how unamused.

Then John Coyle was drunk.
He spilled his beer
across the beige frontroom carpet:

that darker dampness sinking in,
the father vanished
from the scene.

The next week we double-dated.
I convinced John and his girl
to see a double feature,
Irma La Douce and *Tom Jones,*
at the Pines Theatre.

And I can recall John's girl
saying just one thing that night.

After the films, John was quizzical,
contentious, full of ridicule
for movies I had guaranteed he would enjoy.
He turned and asked her
what she thought —
and in the softest
of tones, a vague rumor
of honeysuckle in the air,
she almost whispered,
"I thought they were beautiful."

That was the last time that I saw her,
the last thing that I heard her say.

A few weeks later,
she drove over to John's house
in the middle of the afternoon,
and caught him in bed
with Suzanne Morain,
a graduate assistant
from the English Department at Lamar.

John told me later
that when she saw them in the bedroom

she ran into the kitchen,
picked up a broom,
and began to sweep the floor —
weeping.

When John sauntered in
she threw the broom at him,
ran out the door,
got in her car and drove away.
And from that day on,
no one ever saw that woman
in Beaumont again.

The next day she moved to Austin.
And later on, I heard,
back to San Francisco.
And I remember when John told me this,
with a semi-shocked expression
on his face, he turned
and looked up, and said, "You know,
I guess she must have really *loved* me."

I was twenty years old.
What did I know?
What could I say?

I could not think
of anything to say,
except, "Yes,
I guess so."

It was summertime.

Thus runs the world away.

DOWNPOUR

Kathleen Wakefield

I will go back to the day it rained in the late summer garden,
a merciless rain that plucked my deaf ears
open, such wild applause that had nothing to do with me,
nor the way I'd arranged the broad-leafed hostas
in a half-moon, the laddered spires of lobelia in between,
and then the lilies, loosestrife, and spiky monarda
for rain to fall on, which in the end made no discernible
difference, the whole woods clamoring, a ceaseless drumming
that said, *So much singing cannot be shut out:*
Rise and walk away, and for a moment it was all Mississippis,
cane-backed chairs and spinning reeds, the soft secrecies of
flesh spiralling underneath, but I tell you, it had the absolute
certainty of answered prayer. It was what it was —
rain — having no use for words like *redemption,*
redemption mimicking its course, undefiled by gutter
and downspout, rock and ripped leaf. It was a litany with purpose,
a near monotone that played and leapt to its conclusion
in spite of my foolishness, white flames dancing on a glassy tabletop.
Yes, I know it was simply the result of all the conditions
       that permitted it,
but my God, how it laughed at me, the rain and the green flesh
declaring itself alive.

Kathleen Wakefield

Smell of ash in the air, a distant burning,
and the clatter of wild turkeys,
the racket of sex;
the woods are full of it,

               wing-
tipped, cry of the flicker
like some derangement of the senses, the steering
of fernlip towards the light, what little
we have.
        A low rolling
of thunder and the rain when it comes   falls
like a form of angelic restlessness,
an imagined sighing —
a bitter tonic after a long illness.

Violets bloom at the edge of the lawn
like the purple release of blood
under the skin.
        Kyrie, says the flicker,
all desire and beginning. I doubt it.
This understory of gauzy brush not yet shaken out
is a shimmering scarcely achieved.
              The self
wants to sing,
for who can bear the containment of the trees,
the eyes' aptitude for green now?

The woods are full of it,
rain falling like a part of speech
nearly forgotten,
        like grace notes from a page of music

held in the mind until now.

NOCTURNE: SWIFT WATER POINT

Kathleen Wakefield

Under the starblack and smooth light
the river whispers your names, *you you you*

hushed as the voices of women on the porch below,
names rising like the secret of mayfly and fish, like the silk

of blue heron slipping past the linden outside. Night freighters
glide past on the river, strung with lights. Speckle of moon

on my face, on my sister's white nightgown still whirling
in the room where nails stick down through roofboard and beam

like Jesus' cross. My grandmother breathes deep and low
in her bed, hair like a white halo, and I'm praying for rain

on the roof to shut out this dream where I'm drowning —
He calls me away to that place where the river speaks to me

with its mouths of moss, its lichen tongues iron scented,
bells of red columbine laughing, our bodies curled on dry needles

until the rain falls like my grandmother's words
Before you were born — I try to imagine not breathing, darkness

and nobody there as she peels peaches at the table, fingers
deft as fish in water, orange fish slipping into the blue-flecked bowl,

but where are my brother and sisters? There are so many gaps
and our wooden raft still twirls downstream on a blazing

sheet of light where I left them swimming circles
in an old tin pail, bellies of turquoise and gold that go round

and round in my love's arms, in my grandmother's hands
dripping with the fluency of tears, in the swallows'

sweep and glide from the linden's stained leaves that say
night now; say *sing again*, ships that go down to the sea, rain

that touches the river's lips. Say *mayfly, fish, blue heron*,
say *love*, this breath that goes in, breath that goes out

A REPLY

Kathleen Wakefield

— *Girl Reading a Letter*, Vermeer

If for a moment you believe the heart
hangs on a word,
like the soul on a matter of faith —
that memory or desire might flare
like the red flame of the window drape flung back
into the dark corner, or that this light
surely must have passed through high branches,
layers of new leaves all morning long,

Observe how this outer light
articulates the smooth, high brow
and washes a blinding white the window ledge,
the curled half of the page
she's already read.
                    Oh, it hardly matters
that we'll never know who he is,
or her reply, for the story is always
the same: what's been said and left unsaid,
how the light changes.

Kathleen Wakefield

you have nothing new to say.
Still, some nights you want to dream into being
a river of navigable sorrow so deep
its blue black waters would never run dry
beneath whatever vessel carries you over roils
sudden as your own heart's agitations,
past banks overshadowed by trees thick
and unnameable, though they would have a hint
of light beyond, like the mind backlit
by something other than itself.

At dusk a bird with invisible plumage
would give voice to the grief you can hardly bear
and you would sleep until morning,
the waves' quiet lip-lap washing over you,
over what you don't want to believe:
the spill into those waters, from which you drank,
of a fruit so bitter you could not wake
from its dark taste.

Kathleen Wakefield

There must have been fields. Of those flowers. Blue.
Lupine and flax. Cornflower blue.
Something seen, head turned toward the window:
lace curtain, white shade, the light too much.
How many layers to go through? Slight milkiness
of cataracts, water rushing over rock?
Every line erased, fine yellow skin smoothed
over the high forehead, the aquiline nose.
All agitation ceased now, mask of a mask, radiant
over interior ruin. The body a husk and God
in the eyes gone. Relic of blue glass. Mouth
of awe open: O. The roaring of wind with no sound.
O the shine. Gone.

THE MAN AND WOMAN RAKING LEAVES DO NOT SPEAK OF FABULOUS THINGS

Kathleen Wakefield

Whatever gold trappings the trees have shed
                    they gather bit by bit, pulling leaves from the tines
like pieces of lint. They bend over their voices as if holding them
                    close to earth, hushed, indistinguishable
as a murmur of bees. She imagines a country where the sound
                    of a late, rasping cricket (here, under the still green lilac)
covers the footsteps of a man fleeing. Wearied
                    of her inwardness,

her husband imagines a pull so strong
                    it makes leaves lifted by the wind spiral back
into themselves and go nowhere. Is this sighing over scraped ground
                    how much he desires of her that he cannot have,
or knowledge of how large a world he could hold?
                    In another country, a man imagines
a night darker than coffee, as fragrant:
                    this he could pass through

to the other side. He tastes iron in his mouth (his own blood,
                    or perfect fear, a heart pounding so loud
it could pull the moon into place?) Under the trees by the feeder,
                    the man and woman raking laugh
at the blue jay's outrage: *possess, possess, possess.*
                    Soon they will lie down in the house together.
There are no borders, she thinks, only states
                    of feeling, boredom, fear, elation,

whatever love is (these endless leaves
                    exhaust her, she who has chosen
to live at the edge of a woods). She would like to stop
                    everything and listen: Whoever lies down in the grass
will gain the earth's ear. Bamboo and metal tines
                    comb the dry leaves clicking like beetles

that could live in a desert, anywhere. The man running
                tries not to imagine daylight, blue

that is the memory of something else:
                a song his grandmother sang, a cup
of goat's milk, not this yard where leaves are still falling
                and the sky is blue. The world is so large,
the man lifting leaves would like to say to his wife.
                He loves this day, the trees, the grand
sweep of their rakes, the black arc of hair against her cheek,
                the cricket a blessing.

Kathleen Wakefield

To think I planted
      what seemed heavenly, a drift
          of azure silks,

now frost-stung to darkest ultramarine.
      They hold themselves up
          though the petals

shrivel and furl back, bruised, the way the skin
      on your hands, after chemo,
          peels untidily

to waves of hot pain.
      But what surge of bloom to come: hundreds
          of tightly whorled buds

still rise above the deck rail
      like sea shells glazed with celadon,
          green incandescences

that seem to say,
      What else can the world do
          but consume us?

No good trying to compare your going
      to this near gorgeous ruin.
          Let these blooms

be small Victrolas swelling into song,
      some sentimental tune
          about the steadiness

of someone's love,
      and this tangle of vines
          unwind like one long

unburdened thought
taking shape as gesture,
a word finally said.

Will Wells

Like a shadow, overshadowed,
I give myself to the greater dark:
the swish of cars on wet streets, the long train

passing, the voices through the wall.
As a boy I spun in a tractor tire
hung deep in the woods, and reeled home drunk

on gravity. Drawn out, drawn down,
I knew at last what drove my mother
outdoors on blustery nights to sing

to any friend or stranger on the road.
That's how she travelled, closing her eyes,
as I do mine, turning in all directions.

PICKING THE PEARS TOO SOON

Will Wells

in memory of James Wright

A pear rests in the hand,
a supple stone, longing for
the bruising ground
where nothing proves
solid, and sweetness
rots free of its shape.

Such a drop, before it
falls, tingles strangely;
its secret name is yours.

Years back, I chucked
pears at the garden wall
to savor their mushy explosions.

Now, closing a summer
palled by spring deaths —
my father and my poet,
I sidle up, fearing
that each trailing branch

will break,
a stunted abundance bearing
simple grace down.
I pick gnarled ends
and whisper to the tree.

I ring the trunk
with offerings, so the roots
may nurture on their nurturings.
Grow in me, my fathers,
as I lay the fruit down.

Will Wells

The strike zone was painted black
on the basement wall, a Bible he aimed
intensely for, so the rubber ball
bounced back, bearing a definite mark.

The hours he spent each afternoon,
coaxing his curve to break, a tense series
of thuds. Upstairs his mother
botched hymns on the Magnus organ.

Each ponderous progression oozed
through floorboards, retaliation
to the pounding from below. He turned
the ball behind his back, squeezed

imaginary seams, and caught the sign
from concrete. Then the nod, the set,
the wind-up, and the pitch. No wonder
she fretted over her solitary son.

Steadfast in his dark devotions
while other children played outdoors,
he gave himself to catching corners —
this practiced guile his one vocation.

Will Wells

Each day we go further in,
listening hard for our graves.

We cull the secrets of plants
fallen from the light and compacted
for ages in the earth's deep grasp.

The coal rubs off on us,
so we wear it home like a suit
we've taken out on credit.

In bed we close eyes so tight
the walls come crushing down:
we hear the miners trapped

in our minds, our blood pounding
its long shift in the dark.

Will Wells

Fog and solstice, so I waken
minutes later this third week
of December, the day opaque,
clouds on frosted fields. Sensing
no goad of light through his window,
my son eases back to sleep.

His bus honks twice and continues.
The clock cuts a swath I follow,
gleaning a living from rows
laid out by others. But Gavin
spurns my shaking and burrows
further in, resisting the day.

As he stretches, I hear bones
and sinews pop on the rack of growth.
His lips shape one low vowel
while a muted light filters
through blinds: almost spent,
nine minutes from the source.

He rouses finally to feed himself
and dress. I drive him late
to school as a harsh sun
withers the fog. We squint
and turn our heads, this dazzle
an opulence we can hardly bear.

AN ATONEMENT

Will Wells

— in memoriam E.S.H.

Above the table, to ward contagion off,
an onion dangled and balled a fist.
Like playground bullies, dangers clustered
round your house on Rhodes Avenue, where I
was condemned to dine with disaster.
Beets so purple they bruised the plate.
Bars of halvah like sweetened plaster.
Jarred gefilte fish bobbed in murky brine
like sheep brains in the biology lab.
Thick as axle grease, your apple butter
made me wonder what darkness had festered
good apples into ghoulish gobs of goo.
Raised in a world of cheeseburgers and fries,
I gagged on every course, and crammed
your bounty into my slacks.
                              Forgive me,
Grandma Emma, for all I pushed aside —
the banquet of exile you offered up,
the bloated sour cream floating on the soup.

THE NEST

Will Wells

Like a head displayed on Traitor's Gate,
a bandaged mask woven by paper
wasps is throbbing from the garage gable.

Unsteady on the step-ladder's high board, I
lift a broom to swat that pasty face
far enough to insure my safe retreat.

When my swing
      just misses,
               gravity
clutches my shoulder,
           compelling me along.
Tumbling,
      I improvise
           a triple twist

and tuck
      onto the driveway
               which applauds
my skull.
      Tottering on one leg,
           the ladder
rocks back with amplified force,
           and topples

onto me.
      Up, from a fuddled jumble
of scrapes and sprains,
        I gaze,
           too dazed to move.
Hairy with angels, the sun hums to itself.

ST. PETER'S ON THE MOUNTAINSIDE

Will Wells

Holy stone,
       wholly stained,
              a temple
before the Romans,
         its gods
            have all bled
grapes
     which kneel below
           in terraced arbors.
Though rot
      has scabbed
         the frescoed saints,
the eye restores
       their gaunt,
          ferocious grace.
The oak door
     pivots on
        reluctant hinges
to reveal
   St. Peter,
      who fingers a key
and stares back
     with unflinching
        eyes of soot.
St. Margaret's cross
      has swelled
        to skewer
the sheepish dragon
    lolling
      at her feet.

Crowned
        with a wheat sheaf,
                    and wounded
with carnations,
            Christ endures
                        the cudgel.
Suffering defies
            abstraction,
                    where lambs
are hung
        and gutted
                in the shed outside.

Will Wells

Five hundred years in the making, this
ramshackle Tuscan farmhouse continues
to accrue levels, with sheds and goat pens
mortared into rooms. Its kitchen flagstones
readily compose baroque variations
on footsteps long gone. Burnished flowerpots
attest the subtle chemistry of sun
and time — as art relaxes and wears down
to a more enduring, elemental form.
Once moss and lichens are factored out
and two thousand years of rain factored in,
a Roman legion wends its way across
the crackled contours of a marble chunk
haphazardly patching the garden wall.
My finger follows them to victory
and sentry duty above tomato poles.
Each fruit hails Caesar with its ripe palm.

Patti White

People who fish have a peculiar love for equipment,
for paraphernalia, for spatial coordinates,
trajectories, for the tension between surface and depth.

People who fish know there is more to water
than can be seen by the naked eye, more to a lure
than shape and dazzle, more to filleting than a long
sharp knife; people who fish are patient, dedicated;
they understand the relation between desire and deed.

Down in South Florida, an old couple fished together
for fifty years in the green water of the salt bays,
the black water of springs in turpentine country,
the wide flat saucer of Okeechobee, the sweet rivers,
the brackish mangrove swamps, the shallow Gulf where
big rays come to breed in August, the Everglades,

fifty years on the waters of Florida, fifty years
of setting traps for bait, filling the thermos with
morning coffee, checking the barometer, scaling fish.

She had precise notions about ordering her tackle;
she kept her hooks sharp, her bloodstained stringer
neatly wound and stored; she had her own supplies:
Bandaids, Maalox, Teaberry gum, leaders, sinkers,
ten pound test line, red and white bobbers, Coppertone,
aspirin, antibiotic cream, nitroglycerin pills,

so it made sense to him, when she passed away,
to keep her ashes in her tackle box, for love.

One afternoon two thieves came to the trailer
when the old man was away and couldn't believe their luck.

They came for electrical appliances, carelessly displayed
credit cards or checks, maybe a gold watch or a wedding ring
left lying on the sink after washing up; petty thieves, young,
they came for the obvious, the quick sell to the fence

and found a metal box full of drugs near a rusty bait bucket.

They bolted from the trailer and went directly to Castroville
where Jesus Huerfano purchased the drugs for a reasonable
but not extravagant sum; the thieves walked away with cool cash
and two small packets of white powder for a treat later on.

Jesus made it a rule to sample his product and when he sniffed
he felt the rush, a rather strange sensation, rather glittery,
but certainly, clearly, a chemically induced alteration,
so the drugs went out on the street that evening.

Oh that bone cocaine, the soft ash,
so fine, so white, so

insidious. Two weeks later a stock broker found himself
drawn to the Wal-Mart where he stood staring at the lures
for half an hour, the plastic crabs, fluorescent shrimp,

the Bass Rat, Orange Poppers, the Super Guido Frog,
the Rebels, Rappalas, the Mepps Black Fury,
the Daredevils, Silver Minnows, Scattering Shad,

the 6" Twirl Tail Worms. The merchants in town were surprised
by a run on waders, surf rods, and insect repellent. Charters
rented out to oddly inept men, sniffling trollers whose
needle-marked arms burned in the sun, teenagers
driving BMWs lurked near marinas, and two bait shops
were looted on Sunday night. The two thieves
signed up on a drift boat and worked the season.

And Jesus Huerfano had dreams of glistening fish

skipjacks and mullet, sheepshead, silvery sea trout,
mysterious redfish, grouper, flounder, and tarpon

he dreamed of fish head soup and grainy oysters
of deep-fried snapper throats and conch fritters

he dreamed of soft white sand at the bottom of the sea
and glittering bones that shifted, drifted, so gently,
with the pull of the waves overhead

he dreamed of shining bones
dancing in the current as the fish sailed by.

A MASSING OF PLANETS

Patti White

The screened porch faces north.
Petunias crushed by nightfall
trace sweet designs in humid air;
my breasts are heavy with sweat,
with breath held shallow by heat.

I am subject to memories that burn.

In the west, hidden by maples,
Venus moves close to Mars,
sparking a coordinate fire.

A faint breeze rises in the lilacs,
sheet lightning turns the trees black.
This is the weather of innocent climates,
where climax is gently withheld.

Jupiter swings near and settles;
Leo is crowded with alien bodies,
round and glowing, clustering,
demanding space. Burning space.

Night after night the planets gather,
the heat holds steady, and lightning
promises release. The rain does not come.

The screened porch faces north.
Petunias leave sweet scent suspended,
my breasts hang heavy with memory.
The twilight condenses against glass.

This conjunction ends with the solstice:
A red sun declines, three planets scatter,
wild hours of wind and rain commence.

SHE WEARS OPHELIA'S DRESS

Patti White

She wears Ophelia's dress
wrung out and hung to dry
on the frame of her shoulders.
Or what, perhaps, the creek saw
as it gazed up at a surface
broken, shattered by flesh,
the watery trees and golden herbs
floating around her like cloth
woven so fine as to be transparent.
Had Ophelia lived, she would someday
have owned a dress that, like this one,
appeared as a poetry of thread, a thin tapestry,
a field beneath a face, rosemary for remembrance.

BILLY BAILEY EXECUTED AT 12:04 AM

Patti White

In the seventeen years since the crime
Delaware had changed the penalty to lethal injection
but Bailey insisted on hanging; he said: the law's the law.

And in the seventeen years of waiting, the gallows
had fallen to pieces, so an order came down
to the carpenter shop for the standard model.

When the carpenter asked for plans
they sent him a blueprint with measurements,
an artist's rendering, and a black and white photo
of the last hanging back in 1936, which called to mind
the judge in his robe, crows in the corn, high school
history films of World War Two, and the snapshot booth
at the county fair which was, he thought now, very much
like an execution chamber or something pornographic.

Pine for the gallows was delivered to the prison yard.
The carpenter signed for the nails and the tools,
folded the plan into a back pocket, and went to work,
thinking about a chicken coop he built as a child,
the dust in the yard reminded him of chickens
the thin sunlight recalled winters on the farm,
and that coop, that ramp, the roosts, the wire.

The carpenter was a serious man
so he worked for some time before it came to mind.

He was assembling a platform
and was marking the risers to the steps;
he was sawing the wood and starting to sweat;
he was hammering nails, hammering
one after another and he was humming
humming a little tune and hammering

his arm rising and falling
and it came to him

> won't you come home Bill Bailey?
> won't you come home?

he didn't know he knew the words

> I cried the whole night long.
> I'll send you money Billy
> I'll pay the rent
> I know I done you wrong

his voice sounded pretty good ringing off the walls

> remember that rainy evening
> I threw you out
> with nothing but

He set down the hammer. Pulled out a cigarette.

As he smoked, he ran his hand over the pine.
It wasn't a fine wood, but good enough, and clean.
He liked the feel of it. He liked the grain of it

and that coop might have been pine, he thought.
He thought of Bailey in his cell and recalled
that Bailey'd taken his shotgun right up to the porch
and shot the old folks like a careless hunter, and thought
this was the kind of day a man might have gone hunting.

When he was finished the steps were level,
nineteen of them, the trap door fell quick and quiet.
It was a good gallows, sturdy, simple, solid work
and he was glad of it, glad to be done with it, really.

When dark came the gallows was lit with searchlights
and just before midnight the crowd of witnesses
gathered at the foot of it, keeping close together
in the cold wind, lawyers, cops, prison guards,
and even the family of the victims

but the carpenter's song must have soaked
into the surface of the wood like varnish,

because it came to them, all at once, a shuffling of feet,
a brief expansion, retraction, as if choreographed,
breaths taken in unison, a sense of impending danger,
a sense of the absurd, the spectacular, a musical

and when the prisoner mounted the steps
to have the black hood placed over his head
and then the noose

when he mounted the steps the wind almost carried it
the crowd almost whispered it,
the prisoner must have thought it

> Bill Bailey won't you please
> Bill Bailey won't you please
> Bill Bailey won't you please come home.

Patti White

They take their grieving seriously out west.

I met a man in Spearfish Canyon, he hadn't touched a woman
in the thirty years since his high school sweetheart
ran off with a cowboy after the senior prom.

His momma waited through World War Two,
the Korean War, and halfway through Vietnam
for his daddy to come home from Omaha Beach.

Then she buried his jeans out on the ranch
and planted a rosebush and a flagpole there.

Out west, they got a place in the hills for the heartbroken:
6000 feet above sea level, you look down on the backs of hawks

the Custer herd of buffalo is laid out like a brown shag carpet
and the air's so thin that pine needles fall like knives.

To get there you got to climb through fireburned forest;
you got to drag the dead body of your love up the trail
over quartz chips, dust, and gravel, got to take the pitch
and slope of the mountain head-on, and grab that last spruce
at the edge of the cliff and stand dizzy with wonder
at where you've finally got to, it's so damn high and hard.

And then you lean your hands down on the rimrock
and look over the edge.

It's a thousand feet straight down to the creek bed.

But, sweetheart, you just don't jump.

You don't throw nothing to the wind, to let it spiral down
with the flesh falling off the bone, you don't fling your heart
over,

you don't make a sacrifice, you don't jump, you don't leap.

You stand with your hands on the rock and feel the sunlight
collected in that stone for generations, you look the last spruce
right in its sticky blue face, you turn your back on the void,
and you walk away.

Because grieving and dying are two separate things.
Now you remember that, your next trip west.

ORANGES

Michele Wolf

The cool juice drips loose on our fingers.
At breakfast in the garden, as the sweet breath
Of orange blossoms mingles with the waft
Of wild creamy tea roses, nodding their silky
Heads at us in approval, and the green baby lemons,
Hanging from the tree like gumdrops, rustle against
Their lax shelter of leaves, I notice those
Hairs on your chest that have suddenly turned silver.
Winking, you slide your orange wedge entirely
Into your mouth, then flash me a fiery orange-peel smile.

Fast on the freeway, outside the groves, we passed
A bumpety flatbed truck that owned the road
With its cargo — three car lengths of oranges,
Looking so puckish, so ready to tumble, we couldn't
Stop smiling at them, thousands of flaming suns.
Hours later, from our private perch overlooking
The Palisades, with the warmth of your arm
Around me and the sun settling its vast silver quilt
On the ocean's skin, you told me that, although
You have turned thirty-nine, you still *feel* young.
We have only a short ride on that truck, my love,
A bouncy ride on the truck. Feeding each other, we
Build up the blood and its vessels, sweeten the earth.

TOILETTE

Michele Wolf

She lifts the white, lace nightgown
Over her head, waits for hot
Water to flow into the basin.
The billowing curtain sheer, tulip appliquéd,
Rises with the breeze, revealing
The dogwood's veil of ivory blossoms,
Each with its nubby green core,
Soft-claw edges dipped in mauve.
She washes her face, slides
The washcloth along her armpits,
Between her legs, rinses.
A rush-hour traffic report —
Stalled tractor trailer, half-mile backup —
Radios faintly from the bedroom
Across the yard. She brushes her teeth,
Inserts a contact lens, blinks,
Readies the next one, when an arm
Encircles her waist, a scratchy
Face rests in the curve
At the base of her neck.
Cut off by the mirror, her index
Finger holds out the clear,
Waiting lens to the light
Like a sacrifice. A tiny, malleable cup,
It adheres, balances, preens.
It knows it's been cleansed,
That after its nightly soak — eight
Free-floating hours lazing in saline,
On wave after wave of dreams —
It offers, with transparent
Pleasure, the power to see.

Michele Wolf

The hardest part, in the beginning, is getting down,
In spite of the weights at your waist, the aluminum
Armor guarding the ration of atmosphere
Harnessed to your back. The trick is to exhale
Deeply, knowing the heavy sea is set
To swallow you, that it will pound its bulk
To your ears, that you must shove it back
With your breath, pinching your nose so the blast
Tunnels up through your ears and keeps
The pressures equal. But once you are down,
Accepted by the cushion of the sea, by the salt
That keeps you lifted, gliding at eye level
With masses of shimmering yellow jacks
And, shier, a fiery sky-blue, opalescent wrasse,
Suspended in a shifting Tiffany case of the deep,
You kick from the hip, a subtle effort, using
Your fins plus a conscious pacing of the lungs —
Inhaling more fully to rise, relying on
Exhales to fall — to carefully place you.
The object is neutral buoyancy: to neither dip
Nor climb without intention, but rather to hover,
To pause and remain neutral, at any given depth.
Mastering buoyancy is diving's most elusive task.

The sound of your breathing swirls in your ears
Like the surf's crash and retreat. Underwater,
Time always swims more swiftly than you do.
Checking your gauge, you confirm you have only
So much air. As a child you would test
Your lungs, you and your sister, racing to make
The length of the pool on one breath, then soaring
To break the surface, hearts thumping, chests
Swelling with air. But sometimes there is no
Surface. Sometimes there's only the deep,

That sea where your sister was, beautiful swimmer,
Drowned not by a watery absence of air
But by blood in the brain, brain-dead
On a respirator, pumping her chest up and down
With its loud wheezing: breath funneling into her,
Forced out. Your teeth clench your regulator,
The rubber mouthpiece and hose connecting you
To your air. You stare at the reef,
This risky world that you visit,
So beautiful, achingly beautiful. You start
To ascend, because you are running out of air.

Michele Wolf

"Does it have a spine?" the bookseller
Chided, reluctant to stock a collection
With less evident heft than its stonier kin.

"It has a thin but determined spine,
Staple-bound," I replied. "It stands
On its own. And when you open it, its mottled
White wings will carry you, high on that spine,
Across echoing, dry-river canyons riddled
With petroglyphs, beyond hidden cabins
Dotting tree-glutted mountaintops, a gray spired
City indulgent to street-corner marionettists
And blaring traffic that hugs the square,
Until it lands you, past miles of sea as subtle
As twilight, upon your doorstep, with your
Heart wanting to open its spare room
To strangers, everything crisp."

THE MIDNIGHT CROSSING

Michele Wolf

Your mother had stepped away from the table, and so
Had you. I sat facing your father. Though neither
Would say so, both of us knew something was wrong.
He brought up an article I had written, about ways
For couples to approach fighting fairly, about getting
Along. He had been married close to fifty years. "Don't
Say everything on your mind," he told me. "That works."

On the night of your father's funeral, we drift into sleep,
Two nested question marks, realizing, in our middle
Years, how little life has prepared us for. When we shift
In the night, your hands reach over to find mine, each
Seeking its interlocking mate. By day, on a deadline,
You rewrite computer code. In your field, this millennial
New Year, the double-aught New Year, is known as
The midnight crossing. With midnight's arrival, you
Will discover whether you have missed something critical.

Your father believed in love and in logic, not in God or
An afterlife. Yet, no good at disappearing, he visits
In dreams. "Dad, what are you doing here?" you ask him,
Astonished. "You're dead." "Oh, no," he explains to you.
"I have eleven more days." "Really?" you say. "That's great!
We'll do something. We'll make the most of it." Then,
With a casual wave, your father, smiling, steps out the door.

Michele Wolf

As I was guided by the director through the thick space
Of these rooms, worn sparrow brown, and strode
With the August sun on my shoulders across this particular
Acre of grass, nobody had told me this was the place
Where you had summered as a boy. I have weathered
My fourth decade, older now than you were
When you died. I can barely remember you, yet I can see
You not as my father but as my son. You are age nine.
The downpour divides into two massive stage curtains
Parting. You bolt from the bunk, loudly racing
With your chums down the slippery hill to the dock,
Your cape of a towel flapping as if ready to lift you airborne.

You are the smallest. Still, you always run in the front.
You do not know how beautiful you are, of course, squinting
Against the sun, the flame that escapes behind the gray
Vapor for hours, sometimes for days. You cannot see
That from the beginning it has been eyeing you from afar,
That it has focused its golden spotlight just for you.

THE GREAT TSUNAMI

Michele Wolf

She recognizes its crest in the way he looks at her.
The wave is as vast as the roiling mass in the Japanese
Print they had paused in front of at the museum,
Capped with ringlets of foam, all surging sinew.
That little village along the shore would be
Totally lost. There is no escaping this.
The wave is flooding his heart,
And he is sending the flood
Her way. It rushes
Over her.

Can you look at one face
For the whole of a life?

Does the moon peer down
At the tides and hunger for home?

REVIVAL (FOR MY GRANDMOTHER)

Fabian Worsham

still young,
she lay in a bed of blood:
blood from her womb
        neighbors carried her
        on a makeshift stretcher
        through the red sand streets
        of Lumber City
holding branches to block out the sun
her grey face dappled in shadows almost
as dark as her eyes
        they laid her on the floor of a Southern
        Railway car and pushed the door shut
            o shriveled source
            still you breed us
        for we are born of
        the rhythm of that ride
            the smell of warm blood
            in a boxcar
        we inherit the strength
        of each reeling black hour
the times you felt you lay
inside your own rancid womb
        between the fragments of
        revival songs you
        hummed to make sure
you were still alive
and that this ride would end
        when the train reached Atlanta the door
        slid open and sweet light poured in like
        honey

you would live to tell your children
not to be afraid of death
or boxcars

                for there are always
                doors that will open
                and even in the darkest places
                your own voice will come back
                to you

THE GREEN KANGAROO

Fabian Worsham

Freud, I have often wondered why
you assumed that the female
       is the only form of life
afflicted with the envy
       of its mate's body,
for, as everyone knows,
the male kangaroo has no pouch.

Where the female's body presses
forward,
       full and round, an open harbor
       for her young,
he offers nothing —
       smooth, closed,
       a wasteland.

He spies at her from behind trees
and grasses, as she plucks her pouch
open, checking on her child.
       What secrets hidden there?
       Keepsakes from old lovers?

He follows her in moonlight through
the bush,
       that double heartbeat
       leading him,
until she disappears,
       folds inside herself,
exploring the secret darkness
of her own cave, black
sky without stars, the perfect
solitude of mother and child.

LAMENT OF THE AUDITOR'S WIFE

Fabian Worsham

I should have known better
than to marry a traveling man
should have known my nights
would be filled with old movies:
Gregory Peck, Bela Lugosi
on 17 until four.
I should have known that when I
was just too tired,
I'd go to bed
with a book and a butcherknife
and get up three times
to check the closets.
There's plenty of time
to get the house clean for
the stranger who visits
on weekends, takes a break
from his rural route —
the tired man
who doesn't knock
who goes straight to bed,
counts in his sleep:
poles, spools of copper wire.
He knows the value of orchards
and onion fields.
Beware of the traveling man
who comes home tired, pecans
in his pockets, his clothes
reeking of onions.

THE ANGEL OAK

Fabian Worsham

17 tunnels through orchards towards Kiawah
but off a side road by a churchyard
the Angel Oak drapes its limbs
across an acre of tire tracks

the oldest oak
its trunk too broad to reach around
limbs you can step onto and walk
to the crotch
propped up with stumps
to keep them from breaking off
or rotting where they would have
touched the ground

when moonlight filters through
in shafts between the leaves
it reflects in chrome
and lips and eyes of lovers
who drive out from Charleston

miles from here
farmers plow
to break up its roots

Our thanks to the family of Anhinga poets. Their Anhinga books and affiliations, and where we found them at publication time are listed here.

NICK BOZANIC
Honolulu, Hawaii
The Long Drive Home (Anhinga Prize for Poetry – 1989)
This Once: Poems 1976-1996

EARL S. BRAGGS
Chattanooga, Tennessee
Hat Dancer Blue (Anhinga Prize for Poetry – 1992)
Walking Back From Woodstock, 1997
House on Fontanka, 2000
Crossing Tecumseh Street, 2003

JAMES BROCK
Fort Myers, Florida
nearly Florida, 2000 (Florida Poetry Series)

VAN K. BROCK
World traveler
*Unspeakable Strangers: Descents into the Dark Self,
        Ascents into the Light*, 1995
Founder and former director of Anhinga Press

FLEDA BROWN
Newark, Delaware
Breathing In, Breathing Out (Philip Levine Prize for Poetry – 2001)

CYNTHIA CAHN
Tallahassee, Florida – Deceased, 1984
The Day the Sun Split (Florida Chapbook Award – 1982)

RICK CAMPBELL
Sycamore, Florida
Snakebird: Thirty Years of Anhinga Poets – Editor
Director of Anhinga Press

DONALD CASWELL
Kansas City, Kansas
Three Legged Dog, 1999
Watching the Sun Go Down, 1977
Former director of Anhinga Press
Initiated the Anhinga Prize for Poetry in 1983

VALERIE CHRONIS BICKETT
Valerie, 1979

MARY ANN COLEMAN
Athens, Georgia – Deceased, 2002
Disappearances, 1978

GARY CORSERI
Atlanta, Georgia & Cambridge, Massachusetts
Random Descent, 1989

SILVIA CURBELO
Tampa, Florida
The Secret History of Water, 1997 (Florida Poetry Series)

ROBERT DANA
Coralville, Iowa
The Morning of the Red Admirals, 2004
Summer, 2000
Hello, Stranger, 1996
Judge (Anhinga Prize for Poetry – 1996)

FRANK X. GASPAR
Long Beach, California
Mass for the Grace of a Happy Death (Anhinga Prize for Poetry – 1994)

STEVE GEHRKE
Columbia, Missouri
The Pyramids of Malpighi (Philip Levine Prize for Poetry – 2002)

SAM HARRISON
Ormond Beach, Florida
Okra, 1977

LOLA HASKINS
LaCrosse, Florida
The Rim Benders, 2001 (Florida Poetry Series)

JANET HOLMES
Boise, Idaho
The Physicist at the Mall (Anhinga Prize for Poetry – 1994)

DAVID KIRBY
Tallahassee, Florida
The Opera Lover, 1977

JUDITH KITCHEN
Port Townsend, Washington
Perennials (Anhinga Prize for Poetry – 1985)
Judge (Anhinga Prize for Poetry – 1999)

C. L. (LYNNE) KNIGHT
Snakebird: Thirty Years of Anhinga Poets – Editor
Associate Director of Anhinga Press

P. V. LEFORGE
Grand Ridge, Florida
The Secret Life of Moles, 1992

MIA LEONIN
Miami, Florida
Braid, 1999 (Florida Poetry Series)

JULIA B. LEVINE
Davis, California
Practicing for Heaven (Anhinga Prize for Poetry – 1998)

ROBERT J. LEVY
New York City, New York
Whistle Maker (Anhinga Prize for Poetry – 1986)

RICK LOTT
Jonesboro, Arkansas
Digging for Shark Teeth, 1984

ERIKA MEITNER
Santa Cruz, California
Inventory at the All-night Drugstore (Anhinga Prize for Poetry – 2002)

JUDSON MITCHAM
Macon, Georgia
This April Day, 2003

JEAN MONAHAN
Salem, Massachusetts
Hands (Anhinga Poetry Prize – 1991)

MICHAEL MOTT
Williamsburg, Virginia
Woman and the Sea, 1999
Counting the Grasses, 1980

ANN NEELON
Murray, Kentucky
Easter Vigil (Anhinga Prize for Poetry – 1995)

NAOMI SHIHAB NYE
San Antonio, Texas
Mint Snowball, 2001
Judge (Anhinga Prize for Poetry – 2003)

RICARDO PAU-LLOSA
Miami, Florida
Sorting Metaphors (Anhinga Prize for Poetry – 1983)

FRANCIS POOLE
Newark, Delaware
Gestures, 1979

KEITH RATZLAFF
Pella, Iowa
Man Under a Pear Tree (Anhinga Prize for Poetry – 1996)

SHERRY RIND
Seattle, Washington
The Hawk in the Back Yard (Anhinga Prize for Poetry – 1984)

YVONNE SAPIA
Lake City, Florida
The Fertile Crescent (Florida Chapbook Award – 1983)

RUTH L. SCHWARTZ
Oakland, California
Singular Bodies (Anhinga Prize for Poetry – 2000)

JULIANNE SEEMAN
Seattle, Washington
Enough Light to See (Anhinga Prize for Poetry – 1988)

HAL SHOWS
Tallahassee, Florida
A Breath for Nothing, 1977

LEON STOKESBURY
Atlanta, Georgia
The Royal Nonesuch, 1984

JULIA M. SULLIVAN
Tallahassee, Florida
Drawing: Anhinga with passage from St. John Perse

KATHLEEN WAKEFIELD
Penfield, New York
Notations on the Visible World (Anhinga Prize for Poetry – 1999)

WILL WELLS
Lima, Ohio
Conversing with the Light (Anhinga Prize for Poetry – 1987)

PATTI WHITE
Muncie, Indiana
Tackle Box (Anhinga Prize for Poetry – 2001)

MICHELE WOLF
Chevy Chase, Maryland
Conversations During Sleep (Anhinga Prize for Poetry – 1997)

FABIAN WORSHAM
Houston, Texas – Deceased, 1995
The Green Kangaroo, 1978

"And Anhinga, the Bird, fabled water-turkey whose existence is no fable, whose presence is my delight, my rapture of living- it is enough for me that he lives-- To which page of prodigies again, on what tables of russet waters and white rosettes, in the golden room of the great saurians, will he affix tonight the absurd paragraph of his neck?"

Saint-John Perse